THE ART OF WINNING
TENNIS

STYRLING STROTHER
AND DAN TRAVIS

Contents

To our families, this book was inspired by your unconditional love and support. Allison, Audrey, Everett, Pierce, Vanessa and Gabriel. Thank you for encouraging us to chase our dreams, showing us how to be better husbands and fathers, and teaching us grace, patience, and most of all, love.

To our tennis players who have transformed their practice with us over the last 5 years and risen to a higher level and allowed us to develop the Art of Winning Programme with them.

Thanks to Sean Bell for editing and providing much needed suggestions and feedback.

Preface

The Art of Winning is a joint project that began with Styrling Strother and Dan Travis in April 2017. For the rest of this book we will refer to ourselves as "*We*".

The subject of this book is the individual game in tennis. When we refer to "the game", we mean the individual game of the set. We propose first that each game has both patterns and features; second, that these patterns and features are common to every game that is played. We are also going to contend that these patterns have been overlooked by what we call traditional tennis culture. There is a contradiction between traditional tennis culture and the Art of Winning approach. It is because of this tension and the need for a new approach to improvement in tennis that we have written this book.

It is in the individual game that we can learn to improve. The tennis match provides a ready-made structure for improvement–but we are vulnerable to the guess-work and drama entrenched in traditional tennis culture.

This book is divided into two parts. The first looks at how a game of tennis is won and the features and patterns involved. These will be new to the majority of readers and we have taken as much care as possible to present our ideas. We hope that you will begin to look at tennis in a different way.

The second part looks at our experience in developing what we call *Competitive Intelligence* with our players. Our principles remain the same but we are daily facing new challenges. This is a dynamic and exciting process for us and we hope you experience the same.

We have included a glossary and a chapter called *Discussion for Geeks* as a point of reference as there will be numerous new terms and concepts. The Discussion for Geeks chapter develops ideas in more detail that are referred to in the main chapters. Some of the concepts we introduce to the reader are both novel and involved.

Join the Art of Winning Community

A Free pass into the world of The Art of Winning

www.artofwinningtennis.com

Introduction

This book is based on the dialogue we have had with the tennis players we teach. Our task has been to find answers to the question *"How do I become a better match player?"*

We started asking our players what they thought about playing tennis matches. Replies were varied but there was a common theme. They complained of being 'lost' in a match. They didn't know what to do beyond hitting good shots. It was more revealing when we asked *"What do you think you **should** be doing?"* Common answers were: I need to be more consistent; I need a better backhand and I need a better mindset. When we studied and compared the answers to *"What do you think you should be doing?"*–clear patterns started to emerge.

Players thought they should be hitting better shots, hitting them more often and that they should be more positive. These three things often came together when we were talking to players. If the better shots went in more often then they would be more positive and win.

But how? In a game, shots are missed–then the player is vulnerable to becoming negative and frustrated. Thoughts of losing the whole match start to creep in. We then ask *"So what do you think you need to do about that?"*

The answers players give are revealing and mostly consistent. Players reported that they needed to identify what was going wrong, correct it, then repeat as much as possible on the practice court. Some players thought that this was the only option. Others complained that they tried this; it didn't work and they need to do more of it.

This book attempts to answer one specific question from the outset–*Is there something you can do that doesn't just involve improving your technique and endlessly repeating the shot?*

We think the answer to the question above is "Yes". This book is about the link between good shots, consistency and a good mindset. Our subject has been to examine what this link is and explain it in a series of principles and concepts. We then look at how it is harnessed so you can improve.

We have found that these principles need to be studied, understood and applied at the same time. Each chapter of the book takes one of these principles and we explore them in detail.

Here is a brief summary of each chapter.

Part 1

The book is divided into two parts. The first part looks at the key concepts of the Art of Winning and the challenge faced by traditional tennis thinking. Understanding and applying the concepts help the player improve.

Chapter 1

The Opponent, Closeness and Movement

We look at how traditional tennis culture has focused our minds on technique at the expense of looking at our opponent. We argue that the opponent needs to be central to our thinking on the tennis court. We are much closer to our opponent than we think. By recognizing this closeness, tennis players become better in the four stages of movement.

By connecting our thinking to our opponent, we change what we are looking at. Why "watch the ball" can be very bad advice. We switch from judging our own shots to anticipating our opponent's. Here we introduce the concept of looking past the ball.

Chapter 2

Points are short and First Strike

Points are much shorter than we think they are. The outcome of long rallies does not affect the result of the match. We need to retrain to become more consistent in the first two shots. These two shots are linked together in what we call the First Strike Pattern.

The First Strike sequence is built around your capabilities, your opponent's strengths and weaknesses and what occurred in the previous point.

Chapter 3

Data and Error

This chapter examines how The Art of Winning uses Data from tennis matches. Here, we show how this approach to Data accelerates improvement by focusing on what is relevant to winning matches.

We introduce the *Storyboard of Play* and look at how this helps a player move from match to match. Lastly, we look at the specific events in a game that help us determine what is relevant to improvement on the practice court and what needs to be rehearsed.

Chapter 4

Stability and Continuity

The way we view error is dramatic and we see it as unstable. This view of error causes us to have a chaotic view of tennis matches. This chapter shows how error is stable in both its location and when it occurs.

We show how a change in the way the player views error can bring about a certain kind of stability. This stability allows a continuity between shots, points, games and matches. The continuity is assisted by Data and the rehearsal of First Strike patterns.

Chapter 5
Momentum & Probability
We tackle the traditional tennis view that each new point is a fresh start. We argue that there is a specific type of continuity between points that acts like a legacy. This legacy is called momentum. Understanding Momentum scoring is essential to developing Competitive Intelligence.

Momentum scoring allows us to understand the position we are in moving into the next point. This understanding means we can make a better decision on what to do next based on the probability of winning the next point.

Chapter 6
Let the Games begin
The purpose of this chapter is to bring the match to the practice court and then back again. Specific games that use data are described and are used to build Competitive Intelligence. The games are based on First Strike and Momentum scoring and allow for meaningful and relevant rehearsal of what is to come in the match.

Part 2
Part 2 looks at our experience at the Art of Winning in building Competitive Intelligence and the challenges that lie ahead for the reader.

Chapter 7

Working with Players

In this chapter we look at different types of players and our experience of working with them. We look at the Beginner, the good club player, the competitive junior and the ATP tour player. We ask *"What does each type need to do to improve?"*

Chapter 8

The First Battles of Competitive Intelligence

This chapter looks at how Competitive Intelligence is built. The player is taught to solve problems in a match but they do so as part of a dialogue. We address the issue of motivation and will power and how it needs to combine with tactical thinking.

The question we attempt to answer is "How do we improve the player's decision making point by point?"

Chapter 9

What to do today

This chapter gives you a blueprint so you can hit the ground running. We look at specific tactics for both the practice and the match court.

Chapter 10

Discussion for Geeks

Here we take the discussion of specific ideas that appear in the book and look at them in more depth. We have a more detailed examination of Parasitic Processing, Combinatorial Explosion and more on Tennis Data Analytics.

Chapter 11

The Competitive Intelligence Games (CIGs)

On the practice court, the CI Games are the crucible for improvement. The games are divided into First Strike and Momentum games. We look at each game in order. There are also diagrams for the diferent types of court layout.

Chapter 12
The Glossary
This is the reference section and is a collection of the language of First Strike and the key concepts of the Art of Winning.

We think it is time to move on from what we call traditional tennis culture (See Chapter 11–*The Glossary* for an explanation). We hope this book contributes to a new and better way of playing tennis.

Part 1

1

The Opponent, Closeness and Movement

"You are the second most important person on the court"

Craig O'Shannessy–Brain Game Tennis

If I was pressed by an examiner to answer the question: "What is the main barrier to improvement in tennis?" I would reply: "Not putting the opponent at the front of my thinking". When you learn tennis and come to an understanding of yourself as a competitor, you probably think about your shots and how they can be improved. We may think of our speed and fitness. It's not uncommon to think that we need a more 'positive mental attitude'. Improvement is judged in terms of our technical capabilities with respect to how we hit the ball.

Coaches talk of technical improvement and of movement skills and so on. You get caught up in all of this technical thinking. You talk about it with other players. It forms part of your tennis language. You give it meaning and purpose. But you also sense that there is something missing and you are never certain what it is. Your technical abilities seem to collapse inexplicably or you rarely play to your potential. The antidote to this problem of feeling lost with perpetual mild disappointment is the subject of this book.

In a challenge to the often ritualistic practice court where shots seem to be repeated endlessly and no-one ever asks "Why?", we propose a different way of thinking, or of *thinking better*. We also propose this as the solution to the problems of being lost and not playing to our full potential. We propose that you look less at yourselves and your shots and look more at your opponent. You are lost when you lose sight of your opponent. You lose sight of them in everything you do on the tennis court.

In this chapter, we will look at your opponent in a different way. We will, we hope, start to bring them back into focus. We will look at your opponent in terms of closeness. How close they are to you in the match score and how their closeness determines your movement and how your movement determines theirs.

Our Opponent

Sometimes the opponent is mentioned or thought about but mostly they are obscured by other pressing considerations. This has consequences. The player who places the opponent first thinks in a radically different way. The opponent provides a framework for your thinking. This is the reason why opponent-based thinking can be so powerful.

To make your opponent the object of your thinking, they need to be seen. Most of the time you are not even looking at them and it is no wonder they can take on this mythical, illusory form. The illusory opponent comes to symbolize everything that is wrong or inadequate about you and your game. Because the game is about 'me', I train 'myself' and *I* have to be the one who brings the best shots and makes sure that the technique does not break down. The illusory opponent is often better technically, hits more winners and is more consistent. They are often just so much better. Or an even more powerful illusion is that they are not better than you, an even more dangerous attitude, one of disrespect and all because of the hierarchy of rankings and impressions of past results.

Whether it is because you are not looking at your opponent that you are not conscious of them, or you are not conscious of them because you are not looking at them is a difficult question to answer. We don't think one has to follow from the other. Rather, very early on in your tennis playing careers, the relationship between 'looking' and 'thinking' becomes circular. The less you look the less you are aware and the less you are aware, the less you look. This circularity of 'perception', or in this case a diminished perception, means you lose sight of your opponent. They are not salient to you.

By salient we mean they are the most notable or important. It is the contention of this book that this salience can be developed in such a way that it can be maintained. When you *maintain* you also *expand* and *enhance* your understanding of the other player. This is the meaning and consequence of opponent-based thinking.

You are intertwined with your opponent. You're almost one and the same when you're playing a match. This is true whether you are conscious of this closeness or not. On every level, the opponent is why you are there. They are the reason, the beating heart, of this tennis match and they are inescapable until the match is over. But you consistently attribute strange things to your opponent. Odd motives projected onto your opponent seem to take on a life of their own within the match.

When you have distanced yourself from them, they have a detachment that allows the creation of an internal mythology. Your perception of what is real about the match and the reality of your opponent is at best clouded. At worst, it hardly features at all in your thinking.

This book is a call to place your opponent at the front of your thoughts and to make them primary. You need to keep your opponent first because by doing so you start to recognize the reality that every tennis match is close in the score and this is incredibly important.

The approach described in this book recommends that you learn to make better judgments about how you are going to play the next point. In order to make better judgments you need to understand the reality of a tennis match. In order to understand the reality you need to break through the illusions that dominate your thinking about your opponent that lead to poor judgment about how to play the next point.

Judgment

Breaking the illusions and playing the real match can become a lifelong process as you continue to expand and enhance your judgment capabilities. As we will see, an important part of the process is improving your technical capacities. The process of acquiring new technical skills is reframed in this judgment-building approach.

Technical ability can be improved by the exercise of judgment. A more enhanced, sophisticated exercise of judgment will help you to select better techniques. The more technical capacity you have (such as a mastery of technical options like spins), the better your judgment can become. The better your judgment, the better your technique because you apply what skills you have more effectively.

We may have all the technical skills in the world at our fingertips but without judgment we can't deploy them effectively. Judgment frames technical skills by asking what needs to be done and then matching the skills you already have.

If you execute your judgments well, you attribute success to already having the right technique (because that is the mindset we have) and to an extent, we are right. On the other hand, you will assign failure to having the wrong or faulty technique. Having good or bad technique is the prism through which we judge success or failure in tennis. This is the primary illusion when we play a tennis match, that the majority of errors are technical and are primarily our fault.

When you assess the outcome of a match, it is the technique that comes first in your analysis and the judgments you made about tactical decisions come second. You can try this out for yourself at any time after a match by taking a step back and seeing what it is you hold responsible for your win or loss.

Having good judgment does not guarantee success. Good technique does not guarantee good judgment because judgment and technique are different things. Technique consist of what and how, it is the content. Judgment consists of the when, where and why, it is the context.

Technical training increases the options available but this does not make the judgment any better.

For example, if as an individual all you have in your technique toolbox is the ability to hit high or low, to vary the speed and to hit side to side, you are limited to three decisions on six possible actions. On the other hand, you may also have the ability to hit a wide kick serve on the Ad Court. If you can do this then you can probably hit a slice serve into the body or flat inside. You are much more sophisticated than your opponent if you have these options and your opponent does not. So you have more and better quality options.

The question of judgment remains the same in both cases. You may have only three quality things with which to exercise your judgment but judgment itself is the same even if you have 30 quality techniques. Judgment about whether the decision was good or bad should not rely on the quality or quantity of the options available.

What makes a judgment better or worse is dependent on your understanding of your previous experience of obtaining a successful outcome. You need a working knowledge of the probability of winning the next point. This probability is still entwined with what has happened on the previous point. So you will ask yourself: "How did I get here?"

Good judgment is based on your past experience, including that gained from practice and rehearsal. It is in rehearsal that you gain a knowledge of what you are technically capable of and likelihood of the successful execution of a given technique.

This knowledge is extremely powerful in a match but it will only be available to you if you can answer the question: "How well will this hold out on the next point?" This is the difference between the player who rehearses point to point probability in practice and as a result then makes better judgments during a match and a player who does not.

First exercise to make your opponent the primary focus: Ball-Player

The next time you go out onto the practice court, feed a ball to your opponent and as you look up say "player" immediately. You will notice instantly that your eyes focus on your opponent rather than your shot. Next, as your opponent hits the ball back to you say "ball". You must train your eyes to move from ball to player. Most players do this the other way round or fall prey to the biggest temptation, they will just keep looking at the ball all of the time.

So -

1. Say ***"ball"*** as your opponent hits the ball and then look for the spin of the ball
2. Say "***player***" after you hit the ball as you look up towards your

opponent to see their movement to the ball

3. Move from a cooperative rally to competitive points as your confidence increases

You will probably notice that you tend to obsessively watch the ball as it leaves your racket when you look up. You will possibly experience some dizziness as you recalibrate your vision from the ball to the player. It's very important that you call out "***ball***" and "***player***" verbally until you have made this habitual.

The first point of change for you is to ***see*** the other player. We have all been told to "watch the ball" but rarely to watch the other player. This makes sense because of the way the traditional practice court is organized. Most of the time you are focused on hitting a ball to an open space or maybe a target, instead of another human being ready to return your shot. This repetitive process can obsessively program your eyes to focus on the ball as you look up after striking it.

In order to make better judgments on how to play the next shot, you need to understand the impact of your judgment. What did your shot achieve and was it executed in a way that caused a problem for your opponent?

This all needs to be done in the context of understanding how your opponent moves and strikes the ball you send to them. By doing this you are at the first stage of breaking down illusions about your opponent that will hold you back from improvement.

We then need to look at another defining characteristic of playing points that illusion, pressure, and self-deception tend to obscure. This is the concept of closeness.

Closeness

Most tennis matches are closer than you think they are. This does not just extend to the player's perception (misperception) but involves what could be called the whole of the tennis culture. This problem of the misperception of closeness will become more obvious later on in this book. For now, let's define what the problem of this misperception in tennis matches actually is.

Misperception and illusion in tennis matches come from not understanding how close you are to your opponent. Your opponent is a factor in determining what you do just as much as how you determine what to do in a point or in the match. What your opponent does and what you choose to do are closely bound together.

On a psychological level, one can calculate the extent of misperception by asking players what they thought about the match once it is finished. One of the first things they will refer to is the score. They will refer to the score as if it has a life of its own. For example, they will refer to the match in terms of the score. The set that was 6–3 will be described as a "6–3 set" and one that was reasonably close, somewhere between a thrashing and a tie break situation.

There are two things to note here. One, that the set is both *perceived* as being close and the second is that the score *represents* this closeness. These two aspects of closeness are interrelated and occur simultaneously. They are, for all intents and purposes, interdependent, so the perception of closeness and the score that represents it are one and the same thing.

You can see this interrelation when players occasionally protest that the score does not represent this closeness. In the 6–0 scoreline, for example, they protest that there were several deuces where they fell foul of luck and circumstance as well as where they were not able to prevail in any game.

So there is a sense of closeness that players have. Sometimes this can be conveyed by the score, at other times, where the score was 6–0 or 6 -1, this closeness will be conveyed in other ways, in particular by pointing out the number of deuces that occurred where the set score cannot depict this. In most cases, players will interpret that 6-0 was not close at all. In fact the player will emotionally conclude that they lost the set badly.

In the mind of our competitor, the score *should* represent the match. When it is perceived as not representing the match the player often thinks that some kind of correction is in order. That the score should represent the match gives us a clue as to the way we select and perceive the important parts of the match. Unlike in soccer, where we see the score as a question of 'taken' or 'missed' opportunities, in tennis we see it as a constant report of points that are obtained, usually alternately, until a breakaway moment occurs. The score should represent the reality of closeness because it is the score that is real.

The score in tennis has a life of its own. The score appears to be the match *itself*. This is the first illusion in tennis and one that you need to escape from if you are to start the work of real improvement.

You need to understand that the score is going to be represented retrospectively in the form of a report. So the match was 6–3, 6 -2. What does that tell you? Actually so painfully little that you need to embellish it a little more. But a 6 -3, 6 -2 match can be closer than a 7-5, 6–7, 7–5 match. It may not have been but it could well have been. The tennis score does not give an account of the closeness of a match. A close match can bring a close looking score: 7–5, 6–7, 7–5 or a close match can be 6–2, 6–2 score. Here is a diagram:

	Close	Not close
Score *represents*	7-5 6-7 7-5	6-1 6-0
Score does not *represent*	6-2 6-2	7-5 6-4

So the score will sometimes represent closeness and sometimes it will not. There is not a *necessary* relationship between the two. Part of the misperception of closeness occurs when we let the score dominate our judgment of the match. We also let the score dominate our discussion of the match. This is almost always the first thing we report to other people when the match has finished. Quite naturally, we report the score to other people. The match is then judged in terms of the score and our subjective view of the score will dominate.

The score is the only real account of the match that is available to most of us. It is the ultimate truth. The score cannot lie but it actually reveals very little and hides a lot. The first thing it hides is the closeness. The closeness has its own features and its own story. The closeness has its own context.

The score is a result and not a story, nor is it necessarily the most important match data.

We can now look at another aspect of closeness that works alongside the closeness of the score. When combined with an understanding of the closeness of the score, closeness of movement and anticipation show how you are even more closely entwined with your opponent than perhaps you first thought.

Movement and anticipation

In this section we are going to answer the question "What do you look at when you have hit the ball?" We are going to examine the question of why we look at our opponent and some of the problems and challenges you will face when you start this process. We are then going to describe the stages of movement between shots and how the stages and movement are affected by what you are looking at.

When you hit the ball, you should look up at your opponent as you recover back into position. With almost all tennis players, this is not what happens. Most players are seeing the ball as it crosses the net and lands in their opponent's court. You can test this for yourself with the Ball–Player exercise that we described at the beginning of this chapter.

You are probably looking at where the ball lands and you are probably judging your shot. This judgment is a result of seeing your shot in flight towards your opponent's court. If you are judging yourself (your shot) in terms of seeing where the ball goes after you've hit it, you probably won't be thinking about what's going to happen next. You are not in tune with your opponent. However, when you look up and see your opponent moving to receive the ball, you are expecting and predicting a shot coming back to you. You are in tune with your opponent.

Moving well

Sometimes you don't move in the best way. If you learn to move well, you stand a better chance of winning the point. If you move well, you will almost certainly move well throughout the match. It won't be an occasional event.

In order for your movement to improve, there are specific conditions that must be met. We describe these specific conditions as *stages*. In order for each stage to work, they must work together as a whole. This means that an important part of each individual stage is the movement into the next one.

You need to be in the right place at the right time and be in the right position. So, the right time and place are the first stage and the right position is the second. You then need to deliver the ball into the opponent's part of the court. This is the third stage. Stage four is about recovering your position ready to start stage one again. To summarize:

Stage 1 – The right time and place

Stage 2 – The optimum position

Stage 3 – Delivery

Stage 4 – Recovery and anticipation

How we improve each stage

At the same time as judgment and fluidity work together, each individual stage is improved. There is improvement within and between each stage.

In order to progress our understanding of movement we want to look at the specific challenges of each stage of movement between shots. We can then examine the key question of why most tennis players don't look up at their opponent, why this is a bad thing and what you can do about it.

We have taken the example of the beginner learning to play tennis in our explanation of the challenges tennis players face. We have found that the challenges the beginner faces are still fundamental to tennis players of all levels.

In other words, honing your judgment skills in relation to the speed of the ball and expecting where it is going to bounce is a challenge that will be faced by all levels of players. Using the beginner as an example, allows us to look at the fundamental challenges in a clearer way.

The speed the ball is traveling

The problem that beginners are trying to solve is judging the speed of the ball in the best way to intercept and send it back to their opponent.

Moving around the court to intercept the incoming ball requires one to see the ball on purpose. Perceiving the ball's height, direction, spin, and speed are the factors to consider when moving into the best position to send the ball you desire back to your opponent.

The speed the ball travels is the variable that is most difficult to perceive, it requires experience over time to master.

As a player, the perception of speed is influenced by how soon you see the ball *come out of your opponent's racquet*. Your movement to the ball is then calculated based on this perception.

Being able to recognize how fast or slow a ball comes toward you improves your anticipation which in turn allows you to move precisely to receive the ball more accurately.

This flow between perceiving, anticipating, and then moving is what you want to master over time. When you rehearse using exercises like Ball-Player, this flow becomes more automatic; it becomes more instinctive.

Place, time and position

You want to be in the right place at the right time and you want to get into the right position. After you have considered where the ball is going, you need to get there. The right place is where you stop the ball bouncing twice.

The right position is the best position to meet the ball with your racket.

So you do two things simultaneously: once to stop it bouncing twice and again to be in a good position to meet the ball. Going back to our beginners, they quickly start to combine the two after struggling with the first.

So once they arrive at the right place, they position their bodies in the best way to meet the ball with their racket. Where possible, the player needs to meet the ball at waist height and a little out in front. Sometimes this is just not possible when we have very high, very short and low balls, when they are very fast or in a distant part of the court.

Anticipation in stage four

Whatever level you are at, you will need some degree of anticipation. Anticipation is simply the act of expecting. You anticipate when you are in stage four, when you are recovering your position for the next shot.

Stage four is all about setting the scene to receive the ball from your opponent. Your expectation about what your opponent will do has improved if you have moved into an ideal position to deliver your shot.

When your anticipation improves, the more fluid and smooth your movement from one shot to the next becomes. Better anticipation does not guarantee better movement but it does give you more opportunity to develop higher quality movement.

The relationship between anticipation and better movement is reciprocal. The better your anticipation becomes the better your movement. The better your movement becomes, the better your anticipation.

As we will examine in more detail in a moment, improving anticipation means looking at things in a different way. To be specific, how and when you look at the ball and your opponent and the relationship to the two is important for improved anticipation.

So in stage four we recover then almost immediately (simultaneously) we begin to anticipate Stage 1. We come full circle. The question for you is

"How do you make anticipation habitual?" Before we look at this I want to distinguish between anticipation and speed.

Faster?

Most players and coaches mistake speed for anticipation. Less experienced players will celebrate and remember individual instances where they managed to get to a difficult shot their opponent hit. Moving really quickly to meet your opponent's shot may be spectacular but it is not anticipation. This is more of a reaction to your opponent's shot than anticipating it.

We have observed that you can be too fast from stage four to stage one. To put it another way, you can be too fast to the ball. To some this may sound bizarre and we can understand why. The idea of moving slower and more precisely to intercept the ball will take practice. It is something that you will begin to appreciate when you are practicing.

Good speed and being quick about the court is valuable. Unfortunately, this quickness can hide poor anticipation. Ideally, you want to combine good anticipation skills with speed. Although speed can't replace good anticipation skills, expecting and predicting accurately will help you improve even if you are not particularly quick.

What should be happening?

By looking up at your opponent after you have hit the ball, you will place yourself in the optimum position to determine where your opponent is going to hit the ball. This does not mean that you will be able to predict exactly where they are going to hit the ball. It does not guarantee that you will be right.

What you can guarantee by looking up at your opponent is that you will raise the probability of predicting the place where they are going to hit the ball.

After you hit the ball in stage three, you want to look up at your opponent as you move to recover in stage four. This is why we added the Ball–Player exercise at the beginning of this chapter. You may have already had a chance to practice this. So in stage four, when you are recovering, look at your opponent. There are two reasons you should do this.

First, you will stop judging the results of your shots in the wrong way during the rally. By not directly looking at the ball once you have hit it, you will be less prone to judging your shot by seeing where the ball ends up bouncing. Doing this is judging your delivery in the wrong way.

There is a case for judging your shots by looking at the ball after it has been hit when you are a beginner. When you are a beginner, you want to link your delivery in stage three with the results of that delivery. Looking at where the ball ends up bouncing in your opponent's court can help you check your progress.

As you improve, however, looking at the ball after you've hit it becomes less and less important and then becomes a hindrance. Judging your shots in terms of where the ball bounces can interrupt the flow between stage four and stage one.

The second reason is that looking up at your opponent in stage four will help you improve your anticipation of your opponent's next shot. This is because you will learn to judge the real result of your shot.

The result that you want to see is the effect your shot has on your opponent.

The most important thing that you are observing is your opponent's positioning, what they are doing in stage two. This will give you clues as to how and where they are going to hit the ball next. If you look at the ball after you have hit it, you are wasting this opportunity and you will most certainly react instead of responding proactively.

Finally, judging your shot by looking at where it lands makes the anticipation of the next shot impossible. It makes better judgment based on your opponent's position, impossible. This is because when judging whether your shot is good or bad is based on where your shot lands, it is going to be a black and white issue. It will be a moral (like) judgment of good or bad.

Unfortunately, this moral judgment is almost always negative, it's bad. It's very rarely "Good" and at best will be "Could have done better". When the recovery of stage four is dominated by a next to pointless type of moral judgment, anticipation and a good type of judgment based on what our opponent is going to do next are impossible.

You should look at the ball half the time

Looking at the ball is essential. It's only essential, however, half the time the ball is in play (or in flight). You need to look at the ball when your opponent hits it. Some people use the word *tracking*. Whatever you call it, you need to look at the ball as it comes out of your opponent's racquet and follow it to your contact point. After you contact the ball and look up, focus your eyes on your opponent.

This way of habitually looking at your opponent and then the ball is a lifelong skill and is essential to improving anticipation and good judgment.

Why tennis players look at the ball all the time

In order to make the transition from watching the ball to watching the player, it may be of some help to understand why we think that players have this habit. We have found that understanding why you habitually look at the ball all the time will help you break the habit.

There appears to be several reasons why tennis players will look at the ball all the time. So instead of looking at your opponent after you have hit the ball, the vast majority of players will continue to look at the ball.

The reason for this is that we look at the fastest moving object. The ball is moving faster than our opponent therefore we find the ball first. This is then reinforced when we are taught tennis and are told to "watch the ball". It also makes perfect sense and is rarely questioned. What on earth could be wrong with watching the ball?

When the coach stands on the service line and feeds balls they are standing still. So the student will watch the moving thing, the ball. Watching the ball once the ball has been hit leads the coach and the player to judge each shot. They will judge each shot on where it lands.

The coach may well be watching the player but too often the coach will be looking at stages one, two and three and not four. The coach will feed the ball, watch the player then will look where the ball goes. This completes the judgment of the player's shot. The player will be operating in all four stages, however in stage four, the player will continue to watch the ball after they hit it and look up.

If the player spends too much time practicing this way, they will develop the habit of watching their ball in stage four. This is the opposite of how a player wants to train their eyes when playing an opponent. This dynamic between the coach and the player on the practice court reinforces the habit of watching the ball when the player should be watching the opponent. [1]

---

1 There is not the same kind of closeness between you and your coach as there is between you and your opponent. There is cooperation with the coach not competition. This means that the coach is not as close to you as your opponent. This applies to the practice court and the match.

Look past the ball and look up to your opponent

The opponent is close to you all the time. In this chapter we have described how the score and movement exposes this closeness.

Thinking about your opponent first is the beginning of developing Competitive Intelligence.

The first step in doing this practically is to focus your eyes on your opponent at the right time. We will, for the rest of the book, refer to this as *looking up* at your opponent.

If you neglect training your eyes to look up at your opponent in stage four of the movement chain, anticipating your opponent's shot and timing your decision step (split step) will be nearly impossible to achieve.

What typically happens when you neglect this attention is the chain of movement is broken and you will at best have a late reaction in stage one. This does not mean that you will automatically lose the point. It does mean this lack of attention towards your opponent will increase the probability of playing shots more reactively instead of proactively.

There is a decision step that ends Stage 4 and begins Stage 1, this decision step is most commonly known as the ***Split Step***. As you are looking up at your opponent while in Stage 4, you are anticipating *when* you are going to make this decision step. The Split Step is a wide stance hop on the balls of your feet in order to use the ground force to push into the first step moving to receive the next ball (Stage 1).

The Split Step initiates Stage 1, it connects the movement flow between Stage 4 and Stage 1. The timing of the Split Step is directly related to how you are tracking your opponent's movement with your eyes and predicting when your opponent is going to strike their shot. The Split

Step happens around the time your opponent hits the ball. If you are looking at your ball in Stage 4 as it travels towards your opponent instead of your opponent's racquet and body position, you are going to be late to produce your Split Step.

The mistiming of the Split Step will lead to striking your shot late or having to rush and play the next shot because you are seeing the ball go into your opponent's racquet instead of coming out of your opponent's racquet.

This delayed reaction of your first step in Stage 1 (moving) will cause you to be late in Stage 2 (positioning) and then Stage 3 (sending your shot). The timing of the Split Step is how you create the correct timing and flow between all the Stages.

It's a domino effect, if you have a late reaction with the Split Step then you will have to make adjustments to your movement. This can be problematic as you attempt to play your shot with the optimal height, spin, speed, and direction you desire.

Cultivating the habit of looking past the ball and looking up towards your opponent is an essential part of stage four.

The purpose of this book is to develop Competitive Intelligence by realizing how close you are to your opponent. You have to understand how closely related you are to your opponent and why. How you hit the ball will determine how your opponent moves to receive it. How you see your opponent move will determine how you move to play your next shot. It's that close.

2

Points are short and First Strike

1. 70-20-10 is top down ATP to club

From 12 Principles of The Art of Winning–Art of Winning Principle Number 1

There is a powerful illusion at play in tennis. Tennis players think that points are longer than they are. Part of this illusion is that tennis culture portrays longer rallies as a mark of quality. Longer rallies are better than short ones. This is understandable. You crave rhythm and you have long rallies played back to you on replay (usually in slow motion) when you watch it on the TV. The importance that is attached to long rallies is everywhere in tennis culture. It's in our headspace.

In the last chapter we looked at how our opponent is much closer to us in score and movement. In this chapter, we are going to look at how important perception in tennis matches can be. What you may not realize immediately is that your perception of what is happening in a tennis match is distorted. This is another Art of Winning Principle[2].

2 Art of Winning Principle 10. Perception is distorted by the emotional response to a situation based on current beliefs.

You will quite possibly be under the illusion that being more consistent means being able to sustain long rallies. The more long rallies you have the better you are. This is the first stage of the illusion and there are consequences.

To see what these consequences are, I would challenge you now to look at what is happening on the practice court. I would suggest that what you see is either basket fed, or hand feeding from the coach to player or you will see players putting the ball in play with a ground stroke (instead of a Serve) to rally the point. This will make up more than 80% of what you see on the practice court. What happens on the match court is totally different and this leads us to the second part of what we call the *consistency illusion*.

We will look at how we can develop a more sophisticated understanding of the first two shots that we play and the first two shots of our opponent. We can then look at why a continued focus on the first two shots will form the foundation of Competitive Intelligence. We will also look at some of the thinking that will hold you back from developing Competitive Intelligence.

The Consistency Illusion

"Long rallies are good, aren't they?"

If you ask a player "What happened in the match?", we guarantee that at one point they will tell you about the long rallies. They may well tell you about what shots were working or what their opponent did. But in their explanation, they will describe the longer rallies that took place. In our experience, players give these longer rallies a certain quality. They elevate them in their thinking and when they talk about the match. We believe that is related to the culture of consistency in tennis, the consistency illusion, and to some extent what is played back on the TV. Whatever the cultural or psychological reason, the end result is the same.

You attach a level of importance to long rallies that interferes with your improvement as a player.

So, what's the problem? If long rallies are not as important as most players think they are, then what is the reality? We have found that 60-70% of points are over on or before the fourth shot lands successfully in the court. This means that an error occurs on either shot 1, 2, 3, 4, or 5, 60–70% of the time. Average rally lengths in tournaments, for example, are usually between 3-4 shots. At the other end, the percentage of rallies going over 9 shots averages 10% consistently. Here's the problem:

We perceive the important points to have 9+ shots but they only occur 10% of the time. Therefore, we are not aware of what is really important when it comes to consistency.

And, sadly, the problem gets worse. The data shows us something interesting about longer, 9+ rallies. Not only do they occur only 10% of the time but they are shared 50/50 between the players. In other words, you will win half of the 9+ extended rallies.[3]

This adds to our argument that we are under an illusion when we think about the longer rallies.

So if we are under an illusion what is the reality?

The Battle of the First Strike

There are two statistics from tennis matches that provide the first step in breaking this illusion. The first is that there are roughly 60 points played on average in a set of tennis. We will take this average of 60 points in our example. The second statistic is another average that shows on average

3 In fact, both players could stop the point after shot 8, put their rackets down and toss a coin for the same outcome.

the winner will win 53% of the points, they will lose an average 47% of the points in the match. Using both of these statistics, we will try and give our account of what players perceive to be happening in a match in relation to the score.

In every case, when we ask players what the percentage split of points is after each match that they have played, they will give a much higher margin or percentage difference. So when we ask them "What was the percentage split of points in the first set?". The responses tend to be 60% versus 40%. They will often go higher to 65% versus 35%. The lowest they tend to go is 55% to 45%.

Even if they are closer to guessing 55% to 45% they do not know how many points make up the average set. This leads to the misperception of closeness. In other words, they don't know how close the set is. When it is 55% to 45% on a 60 point set that is 33 points to 27. That is a margin of 6 points. They will 'feel' and say after the match that the margin was bigger (probably double).

Before we move on, it is important to understand that this 6 point margin is small and because it is small it contributes to you not being able to perceive it. The other reason players do not perceive this small margin is because they focus on and are absorbed by movement and, in particular, preventing the collapse of their technique.

As we explained in chapter one, you are focused on movement and in particular the technical aspect or how you hit the ball. We also saw that you can't escape this focus on movement because you have to be in the right place to hit the ball in the best way. The problem is, this focus on movement leaves no room for the focus on this tiny margin. Not least of all because you don't know that it even exists!

So, because the margin is both small and your mind is focused on movement, you don't perceive this six point gap. We go for bigger things.

This is why we call this gap "hidden". When we look at this inability to perceive the gap of six points we call it the *hidden margin.* Dealing with the hidden margin is an essential part of building Competitive Intelligence, which is a central theme of this book.

The different segments of the rally

We have recreated three specific segments of a rally below, or the three stages of a point. Data techniques now allow you to see what happens within the different phases of the point. Each segment has a name.

1. **First Strike (0–4 shots)**

   60-70% of all points played in a tennis match finish here.[4] One player will be dominant in this segment. This section alone provides the opportunity to flip the 6 points you need to win the set and steal them from your opponent. The winner of a tennis match will typically win 55/60% of the First strike points (0-4 shots) versus 45/40% won by the loser. It has the biggest difference in margin between the winner and loser of the three segments.
   We have not found a single match from tens of thousands studied where the match was won by the player who lost in the First Strike phase of the point.

2. **Patterns of Play (5–8 shots)**

   20-30% of points finish here. Players will be more equal in this segment. There is some flip potential and there tends to be more 55%–45%. The interesting point here is that the loser of the match could have 55% of the points in this section. This happens fairly

4 This can vary. Most often the difference occurs when comparing juniors and seniors. The First Strike segment is always bigger than the other two. Please see the 'Discussion for Geeks' for a more in-depth analysis

frequently and there are plenty of examples of matches where the player only won 45% in this section and went on to win the match.

3. **Extended Rally (9+ shots)**

   10%-15% of points finish here. This is the most closely contested segment of the point. It is close to 50% equal across the whole range. Variation is rare. Here, players seem to place much more importance on the outcome than its importance in the match deserves.

The First Strike segment is where all the action takes place. There is no escaping this as we now have data analytics from around the world.

The First Strike battle determines the outcome of every match.

This is why we use First Strike as our starting point to build a consistent and reliable game plan.

Mislocating the battle

Most players guess that the outcome of the match was determined or influenced by the longer rallies. So they think that the battle of the extended 9+ rallies was the decisive one. This is what we mean by mislocating the battle. Players who assume that the longer rallies affect the outcome of the tennis match in a meaningful way are caught up in an illusion. None of the data shows that the outcome of the longer rallies have a bigger impact on the result of the match.

The First Strike stage is the decisive stage of the point *because* it is home to the majority of points played in a match. After the First Strike stage, the point flows into the Patterns of Play stage (5-8 shots). Then the Patterns of Play stage flows to the Extended Rally stage (9+ shots) of the point.

50-70% of all points played in a match will end in the First Strike stage (0-4 shots). So out of 100% of all points, only 20-30% of points will become Patterns of Play points. An average of 10-15% of the points make it beyond the Patterns of Play stage and become Extended Rally points.

The First Strike segment is the lion's share of all points played in a tennis match and that is why it needs the most attention.

Most tennis matches are won or lost by a margin of 6 points. It is the First Strike stage of the point where you can flip the margin of 6 points in your favor. There is no data analytical evidence to suggest that extended rally points affect this 6 point margin of winning or losing of the match.

Practicing for long points

Trying to practice for extended rallies without focusing on First Strike is literally pointless. There is no point because very little time is actually spent playing points in the extended rally phase, and it is therefore point–less.

There is another reason that we think pointless rally practice is damaging to the competitor. It demonizes error. The primary goal is that you need to have a more harmonious relationship with error.

Error is a fact of tennis matches and you are always going to make them in a match. At the Art of Winning, we like to treat error as a fact and teach the player to have a stable and consistent approach to it. This is one of the benefits you gain when you grow and enhance your Competitive Intelligence.

Accepting errors will allow you to move from point to point in a stable and continuous way. Pointless rally practice, however, sets up a battle between good and evil. Good equals consistency (no error) and evil equals error. When you are in a pointless rally practice, error becomes stigmatized and, at the same time, dramatized! Or at worst, error is ignored completely as you quickly move on to the next rally with no consequence associated with the error that ended the last point played.

In this case, error is never dealt with psychologically in practice because the rallies are point less, omitting accountability of results.

Why is it 'Top Down–ATP to Club?'

The first part of the First Strike principle 70–20 -10 is that it often overshadows the second part. ATP down to club means that 70–20 -10 occurs not just at the pro level but at all levels. First Strike will always outweigh the other segments by a large margin. Here are some important considerations about First Strike that are worthy of reflection.

- First Strike is not always 70-20-10. It is sometimes 60-30-10, 60-20-20, 65-25-10, 65-20-15 and on rare occasions it is 55-25-20. First Strike rarely, if ever, falls below 55% of all points played in a match.
- Professional level averages are 60-70% (0-4)
- US College level averages 60-70% (0-4)
- Junior level averages 50-70% (0-4)
- Amateur level averages 60-70% (0-4).
- The average is between 60-70% of the points, not *necessarily* 70% all the time across the board.
- The fact that 70–20–10 is ATP down to club level has profound implications for how you practice. In tennis there is the factor of emulation. You are probably familiar with some of the programes, particularly those online, that offer "Learn to hit a forehand like the Pros" or "The seven tips to make your Serve like X player" and so on. To a degree, emulation is a good thing but it has its downside. In important ways, the top players' Forehands and Serves will bear little relation to the

club players' and to attempt to gain an edge by looking at the pros will typically end in failure and disappointment.

- A player will tend to judge a better player's shots in terms of the way they look and where they land in the court. The better player's shots tend not to be judged in terms of the effect they have on the opponent and the intention the better player has when delivering these shots. So even if you are able to emulate the swings of the best players, there is very little context or intent. *There is also the fact that top players have almost unlimited time to perfect their swings on the practice court and then have tested their strokes on the match court constantly, day after day, week after week.*
- The beauty of 70–20 -10 running from ATP to club level is that it establishes a **real link** between pros and amateurs. Both club players and tour players have to negotiate the fact that 70–20 -10 is a defining feature of *all* tennis matches. This is the real bridge between the elite and the amateur. Exploring and living on this bridge of the First Strike has been incredibly productive for the players we teach. It's like having a wormhole, a magic portal where you can travel from one to the other experience. We know that First Strike has the potential to revolutionize the way the game is taught and played. This is why it is the central principle in growing Competitive Intelligence.

Why are 70% of points in the First Strike segment?

We have examined how and why First Strike is so important to the outcome of the match and why you need to focus on it in practice. We have looked at the reasons why you have to embrace the fact that you are a First Strike Player. First Strike is important to the outcome of a match for other reasons. First Strike brings you closer to the reality of how points are won and lost. It also gives you an unparalleled tool for improvement. You need to look at the tendencies in First Strike; where errors occur and therefore where improvements can be made. You can do this by looking at the four shots that make up the First Strike. We call this the *grammar* of the tennis court and it acts like a new language. We'll look at the grammatical structure below:

The S–The Serve

The R–The Return

The S1–The first shot after the Serve

The R1–The first shot after the Return

It is best to think about the first two shots as the First Strike Sequence. There is the S/S1 2-shot sequence and the R/R1 2-shot sequence. Playing 2 shots in a row which are related to one another in a pattern formation direct your thoughts in a more specific way.

This 2-shot sequencing moves you away from Isolated Shot Making (ISM), playing the Serve or S1 as individual shots, and instead links together the two shots as a pattern combination.

Playing the Return and R1 together in sequence assures the same idea, avoiding ISM and creating a relationship between what zone of the court the Return and the R1 is played into.

Rehearsing these First Strike sequenced shots into specific zones of the court is how you develop automatic patterns.

The S/S1 and R/R1 are the most important shot sequences that you will play because you will play these 2-shots more often than any other shot sequence in a tennis match.

The First Strike court service boxes are divided into 4 equal sections on each side. The Deuce Court is divided into positions **|1|2|3|4|**. Position 1 is the wide serve, Position 2 and 3 are the body serves, and Position 4 is the inside or "T" serve.

The Ad Court is divided into positions **|5|6|7|8|**. Position 5 is the inside or "T" serve, position 6 and 7 are the body serves, and position 8 is the wide serve.

For the less advanced player, the Service boxes can be divided into:

3 sections each | 1 **|2,3|** 4 | | 5 | **6,7** | 8 |

2 sections each **|1,2| |3,4| |5,6| |7,8|**

Behind the Service boxes is the part of the court most commonly referred to as the "BackCourt". The BackCourt is divided into 4 equal sections which are called A,B,C,D. Deuce court is Zone A and B. Ad Court is Zone C and D. The middle section is Zone B and C.

The First Strike court

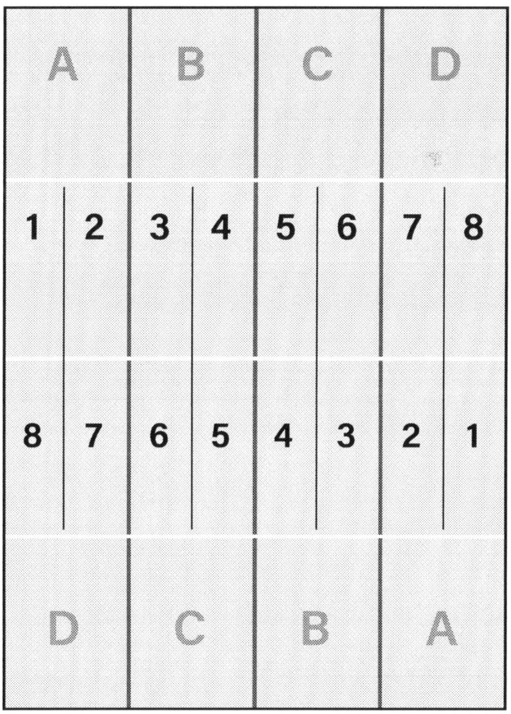

Some examples of the S/S1 First Strike sequence patterns when Serving from the Deuce court can be:

4–D (The Serve is played to Position 4 followed by the S1 shot played to Zone D)

1–A (The Serve is played to Position 1 followed by the S1 shot played to Zone A)

3–C (The Serve is played to Position 3 followed by the S1 shot played to Zone C)

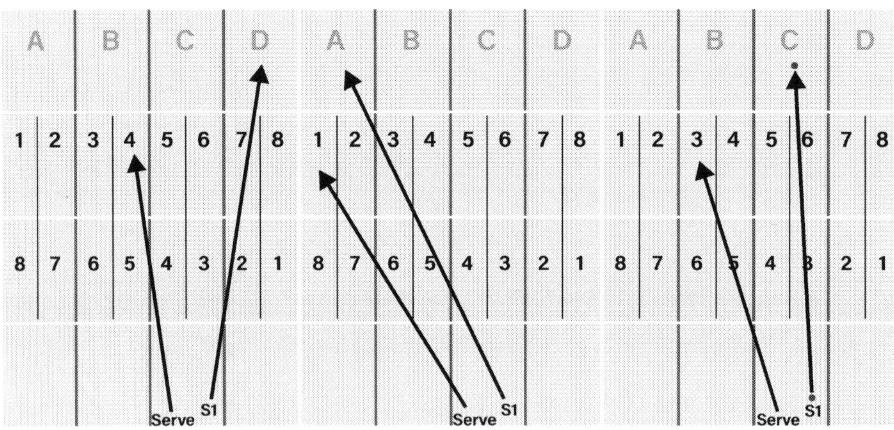

Some examples of the S/S1 First Strike sequence pattern when Serving from the AD Court can be:

7–C (The Serve is played to Position 7 followed by the S1 shot played to Zone C)

5–D (The Serve is played to Position 5 followed by the S1 shot played to Zone D)

8–A (The Serve is played to Position 8 followed by the S1 shot played to Zone A)

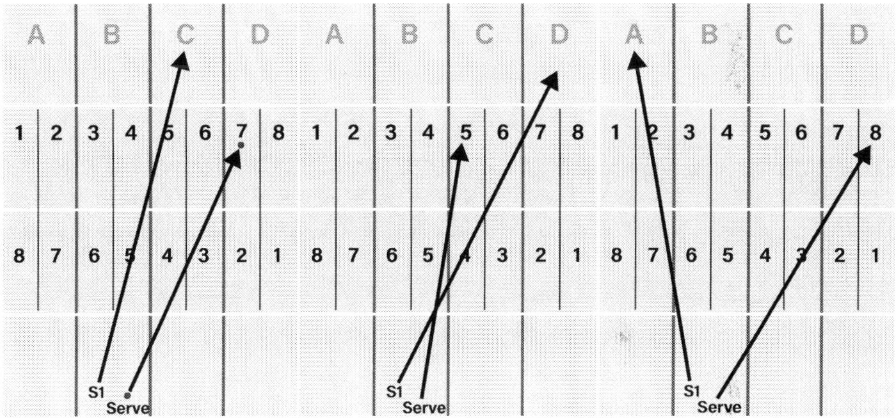

Some examples of the R/R1 First Strike sequence pattern when Returning from Deuce Court can be:

A–C (The Return is played to Zone A followed by the R1 played to Zone C)

B–A (The Return is played to Zone B followed by the R1 played to Zone A)

C–D (The Return is played to Zone C followed by the R1 played to Zone D)

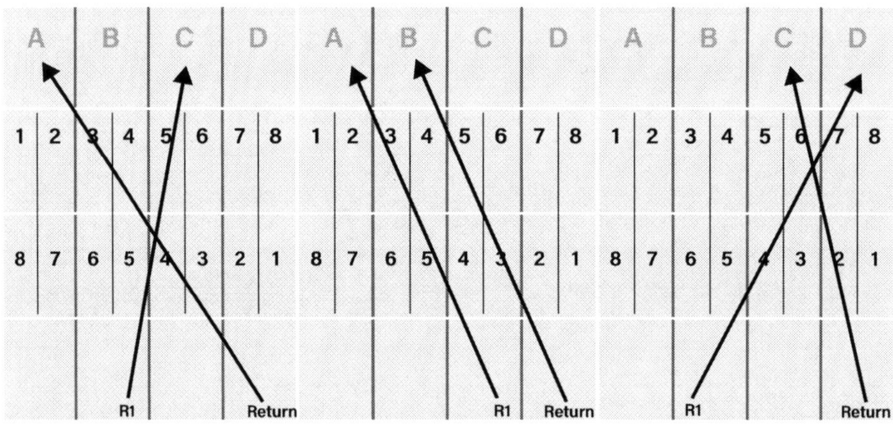

Some examples of the R/R1 First Strike sequence pattern when Returning from Advantage Court can be:

C–D (The Return is played to Zone C followed by the R1 played to Zone D)

D–A (The Return is played to Zone D followed by the R1 played to Zone A)

A–C (The Return is played to Zone A followed by the R1 played to Zone C)

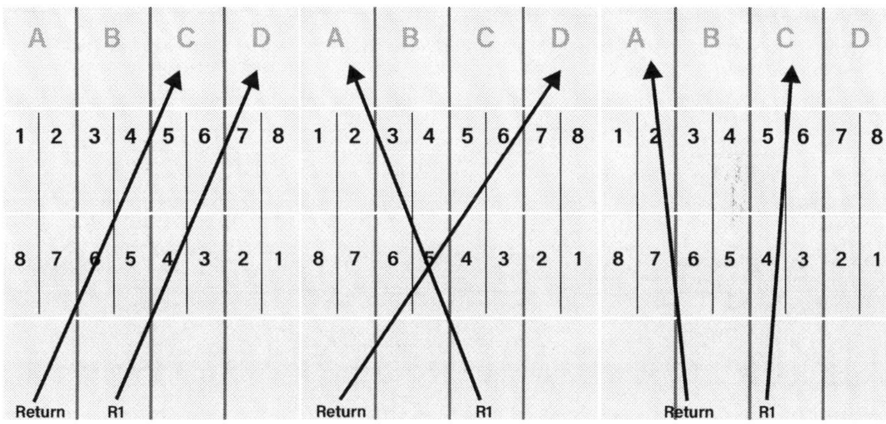

The Errors in First Strike

When a point is won or lost it will be because of an error or a winner. The First Strike segment should be an area where you aim for error reduction instead of winner production. The first goal of every point should be to successfully play the first two shots in the court with purpose using First Strike patterns.

This might sound obvious but players will often prioritize things in the wrong way. They sometimes become lost under pressure and start to think about things that are not relevant to winning. So, for example, you may try too hard and press to hit winners. You could try to put a special type of spin on the ball. You will try to hit close to the sidelines and deep into the corners of the court. You may try to do something special because when you are under pressure, you feel that you need to hit better shots or winners.

If you think that being a good player means having the ability to hit special or difficult shots most of the time and you start to judge the points in this way, you are in trouble. You start to judge your opponent as much better than you. You start to judge yourself as being worse than you are. We call this temptation 'Going ISM', where ISM stands for Individual Shot Making.

ISM is a particular response to a situation. It is, however, almost always based on an illusion that your opponent has better shots and that these better shots are winning the match. You then conclude that the best thing to do is to go ISM and try to hit special shots of your own. This is a form of *checking out* (see Glossary) that we will look at in greater detail later.

When looking at errors in the First Strike phase, we can detect their percentage for each of the first four shots. Because we have extensive data, we are able to say what percentage of errors within First Strike occurred on the Serve(S), Return(R), the S1 and the R1.

For example, we know that on average, 40% of errors that are made within the First Strike phase are Return errors (R errors).

We do not view the serve in the same way as it is the only shot we play that is not hit at us by our opponent. Double faults account for less than 2% of all errors inside of First Strike.

If this percentage is higher for you as a player, it will be obvious where the main source of errors are occurring. But we have found that this is *not* the main source of error in First Strike. We will take the 70% of points that end in the First Strike segment and see how the errors are distributed as a percentage on each of the three shots separate from the Serve. Here they are:

R = 40%

S1 = 30%

R1 = 30%

The above are averages. There is considerable variation in individual matches. It is not unusual to see percentages like these:

R = 55%

S1 = 25%

R1 = 20%

We encourage players who are new to data analytics to record and see the percentage spread of errors being made in their own matches. There is a wide range of variation in percentage distribution of these three shots. The data begins to build a storyboard of your match. In addition, you can compare differences in the percentage error on each shot for you and for your opponent. So your error percentage versus your opponent's might look something like this:

Return Errors/Total Match Return Points	Your % / # Errors	Opponent % / # Errors
35% (17/48)	64% (11/17)	35% (6/17)

Missed Returns

The Return errors make up most errors in First Strike. The S1 and R1 are not far behind. When we are compiling the data, one of the numbers that we record is the rally length. This is the number of shots that land in the court successfully before the point is over. So, if I miss a Return, that is a 1 shot rally length for the point (the Serve lands in). If I miss the S1, it's a 2 shot rally length, the Serve and Return were in, and so on.

We have already seen that the average rally length of a match expressed as a mean is 3.3–3.7 shots. But what is the mode or most frequently occurring rally length? It's 1. It's 1 because we miss Returns more than any other shot. In fact, Return errors account for 25% of all errors in a tennis match. Missed Returns are mostly responsible for bringing the average down.

Missed S1's

Missed S1's are equally as damaging. The S and S1 should work together as a 'chain' or two-shot sequence. The biggest factor for making S1 errors is because we frequently neglect to rehearse the Serve and the S1 together as a two-shot sequence.

We rehearse the Serve in practice in isolation without ever practicing the next shot (S1) after the Serve as a continuous movement sequence. This is a major problem for tennis players when attempting to hold serve, the lack of S/S1 sequence rehearsal on the practice court.

This is why the Art of Winning practice court will spend 60-70% of the practice time rehearsing First Strike shot sequences. Almost everything that is done on the practice court has the First Strike component as the primary focus.

This leads us to the following conclusion:

> ***Given that the Return and S1 are the source of so much error, they should be the first to be practiced and rehearsed the most. The practice court should score the Serve/S1 and Return/R1 sequences and combinations. Scoring on the practice court gives us data and the benchmark for progress. It also allows us to problem solve more specifically to reduce error in the First Strike phase of a point.***

First Strike and continuity *between* points

First Strike training has a dual role. First, it improves performance *within* the point. Second, it improves performance *between* points. Both of these aspects of First Strike are constant themes throughout this book.

As we start with playing both of the first two shots successfully in the court, we then move to where and how we deliver them. This is the progression from *within* the point. What happens within the point can be influenced by what happens *between* points. Between points, there is a selection process, a decision-making process where we need our judgment. When we are serving we can choose a number and a letter,1–D for example (see the chart below).

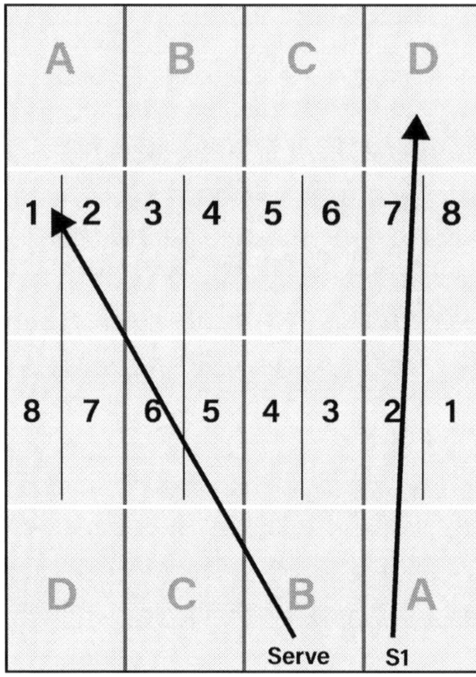

Regardless of whether we execute this pattern, we should still make a decision to play a First Strike pattern on every point that we play. This establishes a continuity and purpose to the way we play. It is a powerful compass to avoid becoming lost within the match. It also leads to success. If you have a target, you will practice hitting it more often. In this way a decision-making process that decides on the First Strike pattern before the point begins provides a frame for better technique and better outcomes to develop. So at the same time, you develop your tactical and technical abilities and you reduce errors during the critical First Strike stage of the point.

From First Strike, all else flows

In the next chapter we will look at a new introduction to tennis culture that has caused controversy and a lot of misunderstanding. For the Art of Winning, however, the use of data has been essential in opening up a new dialogue. It allows you to look at what happens in tennis matches in a new way and allows you to build a new practice court. In a more important way, data has helped us develop a better Competitive Intelligence.

Before we move on, we want to make a suggestion for the practice court.

Let The Games Begin.....

This game is called "First Strike Points."

- Each player can earn a First Strike Point (FSP) when they successfully play the first 2 shots into the court. For the Serve player: S/S1. For the Return player: R/R1
- In addition to earning a FSP, either player will earn the Winning Point as well.
- If a player makes an error in the First Strike phase of the point (0-4) shots. They do not earn a FSP. The Winning Point (WP) is awarded.
- Example score: The first point is played and the rally length is three shots (4th shot is an error, R1). The Serve player earns a FSP and WP, therefore earning 2pts. The Return player is awarded 0 pts. because the R1 was an error, which is the 2nd shot of the Return player. The score is 2-0 in favor of the Serve player. The second point is played and the rally length is six shots. The Serve and Return players each earn an FSP, the Return player earns the WP because the error was made on shot seven by the Serve player. The score is now 3-2 in favor of the Serve player.
- Play each game up to 7 or 10 points, to win by a margin of two points.
- Option 1: Player 1 will Serve until the game is complete, then Player 2 will Serve next game, then continue to alternate.
- Option 2: Player 1 and Player 2 can alternate the serve back and forth as in the traditional Tiebreaker format.
- Play a short set to four games or a complete set to six games.
- You can play with or without specific conditions such as a double

fault is 2 points awarded to the Return player, and a return error is 2 points awarded to the Serve player. These two caveats add competitive pressure to the game.

The objective of First Strike Points is to focus primarily on the first two shots with directed thought and intent. 60-70% of all points end within 0-4 shots so the purpose of the First Strike Point Game is to provoke players towards error reduction in the First Strike phase of a point.

Think in twos – Tennis is a game of twos.

3

Data & Error

The Art of Winning team has been developing a way of analyzing specific events that occur in a tennis match since 2011. This analysis has a framework that selects relevant information on error in the last match. This error relevance has two parts; the first comprises your errors as to when and where they occurred, the second is the errors you provoked from your opponent as to when and where they occurred.

The process of building this framework of relevance has been the result of a dialogue with players. We have moved from the practice court to matches and back to the practice court, taking this framework with us and refining it as we go. Having the capacity to find what is relevant and to develop this capacity is a big part of Competitive Intelligence. At the Art of Winning, we call it Strong Problem Framing.

Understanding what is relevant helps you move past illusions. Developing a capacity for an effective and accurate understanding of what is important allows barriers to improvement and better performance to be overcome.

The role of data is as a constant supply of information to this framework so that you can attempt to play better tennis. In this chapter, we want to give you an understanding of how data works so you can use it to improve.

What is Tennis Data?

Tennis data is a resource that comes from tennis matches where specific events are recorded. Recording of the data can be done in several ways. For example, data can be stored on large computers that gather and store data on tennis matches. Data can also be compiled by an individual. This can be done with pen and paper, apps, or other digital devices. Some sports like baseball and cricket have a culture of data collection that are used to track performance. In tennis, collecting data and compiling the analytics is relatively new.

Tennis data quantifies numerical values of certain events in a tennis match. A numerical value is attached to a particular aspect or event.

For example, you can give a numerical value to the number of shots that land in a particular area of the court. This allows you to say that, for example, "10% of the shots landed in the back center of the court" or "20% of Serves landed in the middle zone of the service box." This is something a spectator would be challenged to recall from memory after watching a match. There are numerous aspects of a tennis match that data analytics can reveal that human memory would find next to impossible.

Tennis data gives you numbers that were not available previously. Most importantly, tennis data allows you to collect several different pieces of information at the same time, something that is practically impossible with unassisted memory and observation. This is not to say that memory and opinion are wrong.

What we are saying is that data can provide answers to certain questions. Data allows us to make better decisions because it gives us more structured information on several different areas.

Tennis Data Analytics

We, at the Art of Winning, systemize tennis data analytics in a specific way. Tennis data analytics have specific numbers that tell a story about certain events in a match. These specific events will occur in every match, meaning that a constant source of relevant data about specific events is available from match to match. This continuity between matches means that we have both accumulation of data and data comparison.

Tennis data is analyzed in today's game and conclusions are drawn from it. The difference with Art of Winning Data Analytics and other tennis data is that our data is framed and selected using a relevance and comparison framework. Tennis data that fails to compare match to match is not as effective as it could be.

The Art of Winning data analytics prioritizes the comparison between matches, in stark contrast to the way data is compiled and analyzed by more traditional methods.

Traditional methods include recording unforced and forced errors, forehand and backhand errors, break point percentages, and many other statistics. These traditional methods lack the specific indicators of when and where these errors occurred in the match. In the case of recording forced or unforced errors, this is a very subjective and opinionated way to record errors. A judgment call needs to be determined by the data recorder whether the error was forced by the opposing player or not.

Although these traditional statistics can be useful and sometimes relevant, they can also be more vulnerable to guesswork and interpretation.

The Art of Winning data analytics, by contrast, examines what data is required before it is recorded again. As we study from match to match, our particular framework structures the data in a specific order. This specific arrangement of the data creates a more accurate understanding for the player of exactly when the errors are occurring and when they are not. This makes it incredibly powerful because now you have a more specific blueprint for rehearsal on the practice court.

Primarily, it allows us to see specifically in which of the three phases of the point (First Strike: 0-4, Patterns of Play: 5-8, Extended Rally: 9+ shots) errors are being made and how often. This is an example of what we call strong framing a problem.

Because our framework uses Strong Problem Framing, our tennis data analytics reveal certain qualities. It is these qualities that make it a capability.

Our analytics give you the relevant information from the First Strike to Extended Rally segments of the point. They show you more specifically what happened within the point. This allows you to chart the match so you can see what is happening as you map from point to point.

Analysis of what happens within and between the points work together so that you can construct a clearer understanding of how to make better decisions to reduce errors in future matches and once back on the practice court.

Ultimately, data analytics provide the information for you to grow and enhance your Competitive Intelligence.

An example of Data Analytics

When beginning to record match data for a player, the first idea is to establish a chart with First Strike language. We are mapping only one player, our player. The Chart is populated from Left to Right with these variables:

S/R: Displays whether player is Serving or Returning

Courtside: Displays the side of the court the point begins

1 / 2 Serve: Displays 1st or 2nd Serve

FS Pattern: This is the First Strike Pattern of each point. When the player is serving, it displays the Serve position in the box (1-8) and what zone the S1 landed in (A,B,C,D). When the player is Returning, it displays the Return and R1 zones the shot landed in (A,B,C,D)

Player RL W/L: This is the Player Rally Length Win/Lost. Displays the number of shots played (attempted or *should have* attempted) by our player and whether they won or lost the point. (Instead of counting every shot played in the court by both players, only count the number of shots by the player being mapped as this is an easier method to count the rally length of each point.)

For example: If your player is Serving and they hit two successful shots in the court (Serve and then the next shot, S1) and win the point, it is displayed as 2W.

Serve (1st shot)
Return (2nd shot)
S1 (3rd shot)
R1 (error)

The PRL is 3 total shots for the point.

If the player makes an error in the second shot they play (S1), or the Return player hits a Return winner (Serve player failed to hit the S1 shot), it displays as 2L. The PRL is 2 shots total for the point.

PRL: Displays the Point Rally Length. Displayed is the total number of successful shots played in the point.

MScore: This is the Momentum Score. Displays how many points our player has won or lost consecutively. The Momentum Score is never tied.

GScore: This is the Game Score.

Below is a sample chart:

S/R	Court side	1/2 Serve	FS Pattern	Player RL W/L	PRL	MScore	GScore
S	D	2	1	1W	1	1-0	15-0
	A	1	8A	2W	3	2-0	30-0
	D	1	1	1W	1	3-0	40-0
	A	2	7	2L	2	0-1	40-15
	D	2	3A	2W	3	1-0	G (1-0)
R	D	2	BC	5W	10	1-0	15-0
	A	2	DA	5W	10	2-0	30-0
	D	1	-	1L	1	0-1	30-15
	A	1	CC	5W	10	1-0	40-15
	D	1	-	1L	1	0-1	40-30
	A	1	DC	5L	9	0-2	40-40
	D	2	BA	5L	9	0-3	AD-
	A	1	-	1L	1	0-1	G (1-1)
S	D	1	4D	2W	3	1-0	15-0
	A	1	5	1W	1	2-0	30-0
	D	1	1	1W	1	3-0	40-0
	A	1	5	1W	1	1-0	G (2-1)
R	D	2	C	1W	2	1-0	15-0
	A	2	DD	13L	25	0-1	15-15
	D	2	CC	7W	14	1-0	30-15
	A	1	-	1L	1	0-1	30-30
	D	2	BA	2W	4	1-0	40-30
	A	DF	-	0	0	2-0	G (3-1)

How continuity is developed between on-court training and data analytics

Creating a transformative environment on the practice court between coach and player is best when there is a constant source of relevant information available from competitive match play.

So many times as coaches, we want to know how our player performed in their last tournament competition. Unfortunately, the impressions our players have of how they performed are clouded by the emotional response to a win or loss of certain matches. Unless the match was mapped with relevant data about specific events (Momentum/Game Score combinations, First Strike Patterns, Rally Length), it's only natural for the player to remember highlights of the match.

For example, a long rally that ended favorably/unfavorably, or a break-point opportunity lost at a key moment in the set score. All too often, a player will blame the inconsistency of the forehand, backhand, or serve to losing tennis matches. This response is emotionally distorted by the illusion that a player is solely responsible at all times with creating the optimal shot.

This illusion neglects our opponent's shot that challenges a player's decision-making process during a point. The way to winning is obscured by the emotional response to feelings of technical inconsistency.

Studying relevant data from match-to-match allows a coach and their players to design an intentional tactical and strategic plan to implement in the next match. This Competitive Intelligence expands our players' capacity to win more matches in the future.

How we select the relevant event of the match

Selecting relevant events of the match are strong-framed with First Strike language. We look closely at the First Strike patterns to establish context for how the rest of the point might have been played. Shot momentum is established or disrupted within the first two shots and then continues into the next phase of the point, Patterns of Play (5-8 shots).

The First Strike pattern with which you begin the point will result in the probability of winning that point. Your negotiation is centered around your decision-making with regards to shot selection, targets, and aggressiveness. When looking at the mapping chart below, we can clearly see our player when serving establishes a Serve position pattern in the Deuce and Ad Courts. In the first serve game our player chose to hit Position 1 (wide Deuce court) on the first two points from Deuce Court.

Serve Game 1

S/R	Court side	1/2 Serve	FS Pattern	Player RL W/L	PRL	MScore	GScore
S	D	2	1	1W	1	1-0	15-0
	A	1	8A	2W	3	2-0	30-0
	D	1	1	1W	1	3-0	40-0
	A	2	7	2L	2	0-1	40-15
	D	2	3A	2W	3	1-0	G (1-0)

Both serves resulted in a Return error from the opponent. Taking a closer look at what Serve positions were chosen by our player in the AD Court, both were Serves to their opponent's backhand. Wide to Position 8 (Game Point #2) and then into the body backhand side to Position 7 (Game Point #4). And then the final point of the game (Game Point #5), the Serve was played to Position 3 on the Deuce Court, a body serve to the backhand side of their opponent (opponent was a right-handed player).

S/R	Court side	1/2 Serve	FS Pattern	Player RL W/L	PRL	MScore	GScore
S	D	2	1	1W	1	1-0	15-0
	A	1	8A	2W	3	2-0	30-0
	D	1	1	1W	1	3-0	40-0
	A	2	7	2L	2	0-1	40-15
	D	2	3A	2W	3	1-0	G (1-0)

Identifying the type of relevant data to map creates a framework that structures the data in a storyboard format to examine. So as we look at the first service game of our player above, it is clear our player's decisions were not random, emotional decisions based on the Game Score alone. These Serve positions are pre-planned before the match begins and therefore creates a solid foundational pattern to avoid becoming lost in the match.

Let's look now at the second Serve Game of our player and the serve positions in Deuce and Ad courts. In the Deuce court, our player begins with an inside serve, position 4 on the first point of the game. This is a brilliant choice because it assumes the opponent is expecting an outside or wide serve, position 1, as in the first game of the match. Then, on the next point served to Deuce court, our player hits to position 1. This is the foundational serve position that was established in Game 1 of the match.

Serve Game 2

S	D	1	4D	2W	3	1-0	15-0
	A	1	5	1W	1	2-0	30-0
	D	1	1	1W	1	3-0	40-0
	A	1	5	1W	1	1-0	G (2-1)

Now, our player's Serve positions on the AD Court for the second and fourth points of the game are similar to the Deuce Court positions. In the first game, our player served Positions 8 and 7 (wide serves) on the AD Court. In this second service game, our player decides to play Position 5 (inside or T-serve).

Contrasting the two Serve games by our player, it is clear these decisions were intentionally designed to create stability in the decision-making process as well as probing for their opponent's Return tendencies.

S	D	1	4D	2W	3	1-0	15-0
	A	1	5	1W	1	2-0	30-0
	D	1	1	1W	1	3-0	40-0
	A	1	5	1W	1	1-0	G (2-1)

After studying the first two Serve games of our player, the Serve positions are deliberate, well-planned, and establish patterns that will offer the player continued stability throughout the match.

What the numbers say

Comparing and contrasting data analytics from match to match creates continuity in the conversations around improving competitiveness. Technique is discussed in the context of tactical pattern choice and application in specific scoring situations. For example, our player's First Strike pattern should be slightly different when the score is (2-0) 30-30 versus (0-2) 30-30.

The Momentum score will reveal two different probabilities for 30-30 in this example. (2-0) 30-30, a player will start with a 25% probability of winning the 3rd point in a row. (0-2) 30-30, a player will start with a 75% probability of winning just one point next. Both of these scoring scenarios will have to be navigated by slightly different decisions of how and where to play the First Strike sequence. This begins with an understanding that 30-30 is not tied when the probability of who wins the next point is considered; it is not 50/50. In fact there is a stark contrast with these two scoring scenarios when the Momentum score is included. This is what's so powerful about the Momentum score.

The Momentum score reveals the starting probability or chance of continually winning consecutive points and sustaining momentum as opposed to winning one point to disrupt momentum.

How we record data and present it to a player

The Art of Winning data analytics are collected and recorded in several different ways. We use customized mapping charts that produce a Competitive Intelligence Report (CIR) which is generated with computer software developed at the Art of Winning. We typically present the data to our players in person or by video call using any match video available along with the CIR. Our app called Tennis MapPlay has been re-engineered to reflect these updated changes in our mapping charts. Check out the new version of Tennis MapPlay in the App Store.

Data Analytics, language and improving the Storyboard of Play

In order to expand and enhance your competitive intelligence you need a language, a grammar, in which you can organize your thoughts and have a dialogue with others. This language and grammar works two ways simultaneously. Because it is a language it must, by definition, be used by other people. Language is social and uses meaning structured through grammar. In the case of competitive intelligence the language is of First Strike. To any outsider, the language of First Strike is difficult to understand at the beginning. With any language over time, it becomes more fluid and effective in communicating and articulating information.

On the other hand, tennis culture has always tended to speak in the language of observation and assumption. It is quite a priestly language. It refers to ritual and received wisdom. Superstition, expert knowledge and opinion are its features. This language of ritual and received wisdom is the language of tennis and its teaching. We are comfortable with it but it is partly responsible for players becoming lost in a tennis match and simply not knowing what to do. This is in contrast with the First Strike language at the Art of Winning.

First Strike is a language of precision. It relies on data analytics from previous matches so that you can then decide what they mean and how to apply them to the practice court and the next match. With this type of precision you increase the probability of winning the next match.

First Strike is also a language of purpose. It is deliberate. You talk in First Strike because you want to grow and improve as a tennis player. You speak in First Strike because you know that reducing error is your main task and that other people understand that too. It closes the gap between coach and player, the coach who gives opinions, and the player who receives them. This gap is closed with First Strike because the coach and player are talking about the same thing.

The replacement of opinion and acceptance with purpose, precision, and fact completely resets and revolutionizes the relationship between player and coach. (Continued in the Geeks section)

The Specific Events of Tennis Data Analytics

The specific data that we use in our Data Analytics are as follows:

Rally Length

This is the number of shots that successfully land in the court. We know that 60-70% of all points on average will end 0-4 shots. The primary job of mapping rally length is to determine the outcome of the First Strike segment battle. You can determine the percentage relationship of winning points inside the First Strike phase between the players.

For example: 67% of all the points played in the match ended in the First

Strike phase. Out of the 100% of those First Strike points, John won 56% of those points that ended 0-4 shots while his opponent won 44%. Therefore we can say with confidence that John won the First Strike battle.

This then allows us to see where the majority of points were played and have a framework for understanding why and how these First Strike points were won or lost. We can also conclude with a great amount of certainty without looking at the 33% of the remaining points in the match that John most certainly won this match. Why? Because even if John's opponent won the majority of 5+ rally length points, the majority of points were played in the First Strike phase which John had +12% advantage.

First Strike Shot combinations

The First Strike shot combinations are divided into Serve and Return sequences. So you have a number on the Serve followed by Forehand or Backhand (abbreviated to FH or BH). As an example, these First Strike sequences would be represented as "1 FH" or "7 BH". On the return you have FH–BH , FH–FH BH–BH or BH–FH. Here are two relevant events that consistently occur where we want specific data, the S/ S1 and R/R1 First Strike Sequence Combinations.

First, we want to look for what creates the opportunity to play a Forehand on the S1 or R1. When you are serving, you will hit zones 1–8 (see below). Your opponent then plays their Return and you may have the opportunity to hit a Forehand. Hitting a forehand on the S1 when Serving and R1 when Returning is the desired outcome.[5] We want to see which zone you hit on the Serve that can prompt the Return player giving you the opportunity to hit a Forehand on the S1 and which zone gives you a Forehand opportunity.

---

5 Please see the Discussion for Geeks on the benefits and desirability of creating the opportunity to hit a forehand on the S1 and R1 - ***The First Strike Forehand***

Second, we want to see the winning percentage on the different combinations so we can compare them. For example, you can see that you won the point 70% of the time when you hit two consecutive Forehands when Returning your opponent's Serve (FH–FH). In comparison, you won 35% of the points when your combination was two consecutive Backhands when Returning your opponent's Serve (BH–BH).

First Strike Pattern

Again, this is divided into Serve and Return. The difference between the First Strike shot combination and the First Strike pattern is that the latter tells us in which zone each of the shots landed. So the two shot patterns on the Serve will be described as 4-D from Deuce Court or 8-A from Ad Court.

Deuce Court (S/S1) 4D

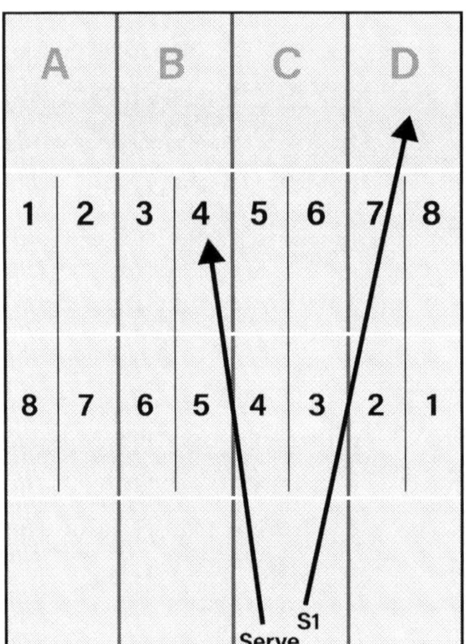

Ad Court (S/S1) 8A

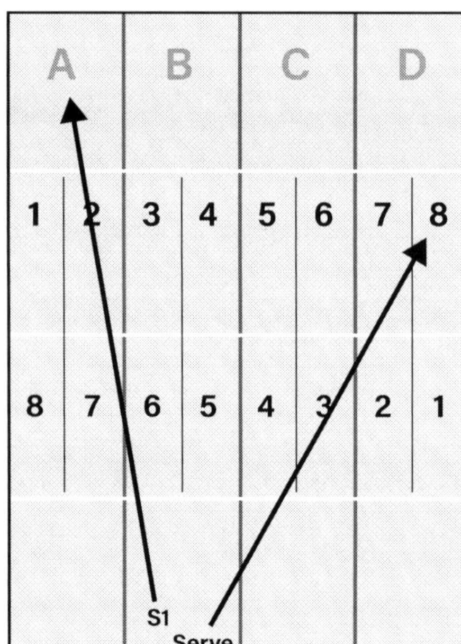

For the return, the description would look like A-C from Deuce Court, C-D from Ad Court. The primary purpose of this data is that it shows you where both your errors and your opponents' errors are made. It will show you your strongest combinations and it will show your opponent's weakest (on that particular occasion). Crucially, it helps us think about our opponent. You establish a way of talking about your opponent in terms of the First Strike patterns that may be most effective against them.

Deuce Court (R/R1) AC

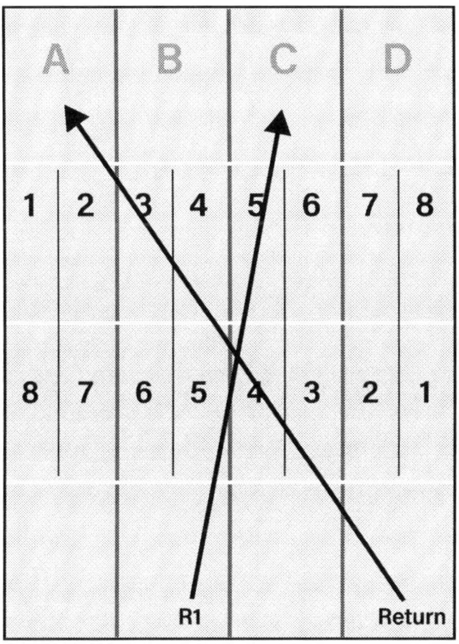

Ad Court (R/R1) CD

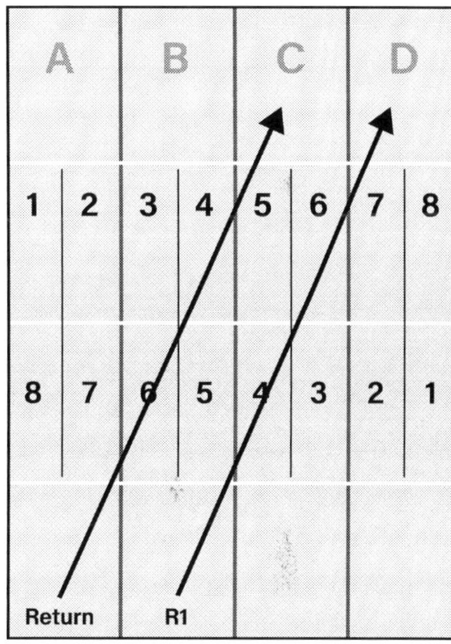

Momentum Score

Here we are looking at the flow of points between players. So we plot the flow of points on a graph. This allows us to see what happens when you are behind one, two or three points. It has also allowed us to establish the probabilities of what will happen on the next point between players. The probability rises depending on how many points you have lost sequentially. So if you have lost 2 points in a row, the probability of you winning the next point is higher. We will explore this more in Chapter 5 on *Momentum and Probability*.

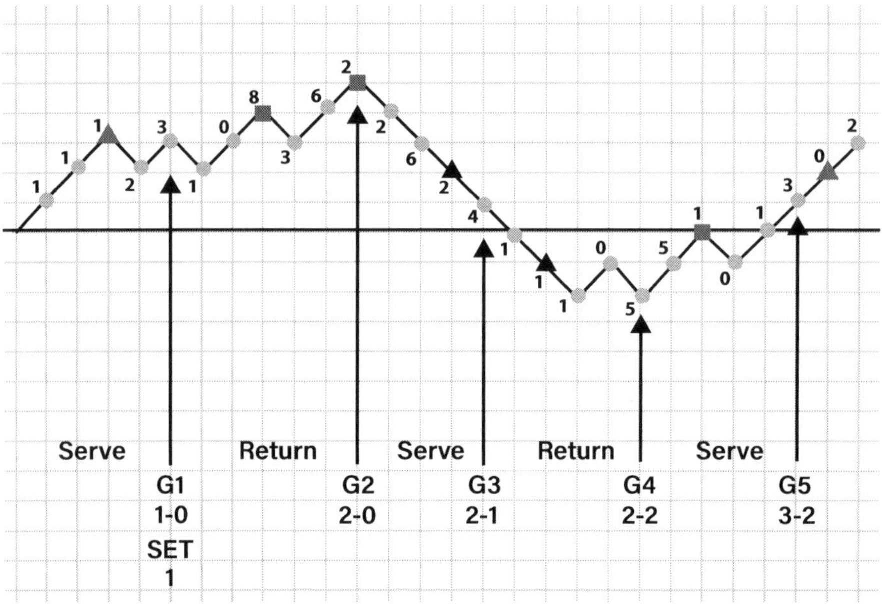

Tennis matches are seen as chaotic and error as random

The contrast between the First Strike language and traditional tennis consciousness is made clearer by looking at our attitude towards error. Traditional tennis thinking sees tennis matches in many ways as chaotic with errors scattered throughout the 3 stages of a point equally. The probability of errors happening more often in the First Strike stage than the other stages of the point is often overlooked and ignored. Considering errors as random does not help a player mentally negotiate with the probability of winning or losing points consecutively. This can also contribute to a sense of being lost and unable to stabilize themselves in order to make better decisions moving forward.

Random errors and luck are often mentioned in the same sentence. After all, people do say "Better luck next time" a lot in tennis.You find that matches are described in terms of technical breakdown and a lack of positive thinking. This just adds to the view of a match as both too complex and chaotic. It is so imprecise, impressionistic and temporary that it can be repeated again and again and you can carry on in a ritualistic way forever. [6]

The use of data and the First Strike language is the opposite to this chaotic, random view. Errors in a tennis match are not random or chaotic. The errors are specific and they are localized. The same patterns emerge again and again in the same areas.

When we use the data we are looking for a greater precision and to be able to see precisely where the error occurs in the rally.

You want to know how many of the 15 -15 points were won or lost and if one First Strike pattern was more successful than another. You already know in this example that the 15–15 point will be played on the right, on the Deuce court. You can then look at the data to spot patterns. You will know from momentum scoring data whether the player won or lost the previous point. If you are Serving, you can see what sequences you have used. You'll know what the win ratio is when the score is 15 all.

Even better, you will crucially be able to tell what your win/loss percentage was when the score was 15 all and you lost the previous point, and the same when you won the previous point. You will be able to look at the First Strike Combinations you used when you were a point ahead and when you were a point behind. That precision, that data analytics is a powerful tool for improvement and central to Competitive Intelligence.

Continuity and stability with First Strike Data

When data and First Strike awareness work together, they allow for growth and improvement. This is because they provide a relationship with reality that is more effective than the traditional way of coaching. This reality is that most of the action begins and ends with the first four

6 For a look at what happens with misdiagnosis of the problem see–The Player

shots of a point. This data-awareness relationship can be articulated and improved. You can measure and compare to quantify improvement. There is an inherent stability to data analytics and the First Strike awareness that promotes continuity.

Data analytics is the antidote to the confusion and apparent chaos in a tennis match. The traditional approach of guessing or speculating when and why error occurs simply leads a player to continually misinterpret error. Using data to understand that error is localized instead of being random completely transforms the relationship to error. It defines what needs to happen on the practice court.

Traditional thinking dramatizes error, randomly criminalizing it as if it can strike at any moment. First Strike awareness identifies error and data is used to build a description of error in a new way.

Monitoring error

Data can build a picture of closeness in a way that opinion and observation cannot. It helps build a storyboard of play. Data is also important in understanding context and the way that closeness unfolds. Ultimately, data assists us in strong-framing problems. This is extremely important when we seek to improve.

The storyboard of the match is an unfolding tale of closeness. The actors will both play their parts. The most valuable data is when the error occurred, where it occurred. and on which type of shot.

When we look at technical errors, why do we not have these extra dimensions? Errors might result from technical execution but the information will only ever be damagingly partial. If we are to make full use of the potential of data we need to use it directly to strong-frame the problem, instead of simply using data to point out a technical flaw.

Strong-framing allows us to intelligently create and recreate on the practice court. Strong-framing the practice court is a dynamic process enhanced by new data at every session. In this sense, the practice court is renewed and comes alive, based on previous matches with data that then feeds into the next match.

Data is a report on closeness

Data in tennis can report on the number of shots made, the type of shots made (FH,BH, volley) and where the shots were played. It can work with the score and provide information about how many game points were won with a Forehand. Crucially, data indicates what you should do to improve the probability of winning the next point when momentum scoring is used.

Data's relationship to probability helps us understand closeness. Data gives us a report from a match allowing us to make specific alterations to the practice court.

By identifying what we need to rehearse, we improve for the next. The cycle of data, then rehearsal, then match play begins again. What happens in 99% of cases is that the practice court is based on opinion about what is wrong or lacking. 99% of the time it is seen as technique breaking down and manifests itself as inconsistency.

Under these circumstances, the rehearsal court or practice sessions are identical and never change. They become a safe space and are ritualistic. Extended rallying becomes a feature.

The technical response to the opinion or observation of what is happening dominates the traditional practice court. This means there are continual safe and ritualistic repetitions of perceived technical and consistency problems. Consistency is seen as consistency of technique. With no feedback from matches (the coach rarely watches matches), the loop begins again.

Where the data is less defined is on the technical side. Technical or technique data can be very useful but it needs ***context*** in order to improve a winning match percentage.

Technical data looks at the movement of a player, a different type of data that has a more biological slant, with outcome data and execution data. Tennis is culturally obsessed with execution and technique. The role that the technique plays in improvement is debatable and yet it dominates the practice court. It is the first thing that players and coaches look at when seeking improvement. It is seen as the exclusive goal of improvement. We think that this dominance of technique has generally had a negative effect on tennis as a sport and will be discussed in more detail later.

Technical data tends to feed back into the technique dominated loop. More technical data means more technical analysis and the domination of technique continues.

When?

The when aspect of data is particularly important as this makes a story. A story needs a when. Without a when we are left with opinion and a fatally overgeneralized impression of the problem. When the error occurs is essential to the plot and to the strong-framing of the practice court. The when is very specific: on what point in the game; what happened on the previous point and on which shot of the point? These three whens are crucial to story-boarding and strong-frame building.

Objections to a data led approach

People have a problem with using data in tennis and there are several aspects to it. At the heart of the problem there is a deep unease with the idea of judgment and of making judgements. Making anything other than technical judgments is seen as off limits. It ruptures the safe space. Technical judgements are safe judgements. They have no end to them. They seem to be part of a story but are not really a story at all.

Technical judgements have no ***when*** to them. They are based mostly on opinions which can fluctuate from person to person. Data judges directly what happened (FH error), when it happened, and how often. Data can identify patterns that repeat or change, which can lead to better decision making processes and identify probability of error from point to point.

Without the use of frequent and relevant data, we continue with what we are comfortable with; mindless, pleasant and ritualistic repetition. This is the safe space that we hide in. Many coaches are hesitant to modify the practice court as it may lose a comfortable repetitive structure where players feel less pressure and accountability when making errors.

When practice is not scored, and the mindless hitting of ball after ball is exercised, pressure is reduced and the practice rehearsal of shots lack the type of accountability demanded in match play.

It is true that extended rally practice produces a flow that makes a player feel comfortable with their consistency. However, in competitive match play where the score is being kept, a much different flow exists where points become shorter and pressure increases as a player must manage the stopping and starting again from point to point. Many coaches fear the loss of revenue if they lose a student because they fail to make the player comfortable in practice. They also get stuck in the loop [7] .

The data-led approach requires the player to play a match. For many people, playing matches is terrifying and outside the safe space of perpetual technical training. This is so common that more tennis is played on the practice court (coaching and hitting) than it is playing matches. This is a damaging imbalance; no matches, no data. This leads to a dull practice court with the repetition of technical adjustments.

The purpose of data is to assist in analysis that can lead to better judgment. Part of living in the tennis court safe space is to see the outcome of points

---

7 Please see the essay on 'The Player' that is in the Geeks section.

as unpredictable. If one is of the mindset that all one can do is make technical and consistency improvements then one is not well disposed to making tactical interventions.

Attempts at tactical intervention are dramatically improved with the use of data.

This is because we get a much better picture of probability and we improve the quality of prediction. We get a temporal, moment-to-moment view of closeness. Because we have a better story, prediction is possible. The practice court is strong-framed and probability awareness assists effective prediction. All this helps build confidence. Confidence in the data leads to confidence in the analysis of probability and then on to confidence in the prediction.

Those who reject data seem adverse to this confidence. They will point out that you are looking for a certainty that does not exist. Ultimately, they claim, the outcome is both unpredictable and uncertain. Thus the safe space of the ritualized practice court continues.

4

Stability and Continuity

The Stability of Error

The essence of Competitive Intelligence is that it frees up your mind to see your opponent as they are, how we overcome the challenges they set us and how we fruitfully challenge them.

In this chapter we want to demonstrate the instability of the traditional way that error is perceived and dealt with. This is not easy. We want to take care in the way we present our concept, presenting it gradually in the hope that its complexity doesn't confuse. We'll start with a summary of the argument and then look at it in stages.

Our starting point is:

The way you imagine a tennis match is tied to the way you understand error[8]

The traditional concept of error in a tennis match is that errors are seen as occurring randomly. They are also seen as both invasive and chaotic.

8 To *perceive* is to become aware of something directly through the senses. To *conceive* is to form something in the mind or to develop an understanding.

This traditional concept of the tennis match goes further. Because errors are perceived as random, invasive and chaotic, then all matches are seen this way. We argue that, contrary to this traditional view of the randomness of errors in a tennis match, errors are localized and stable. When error is misdiagnosed, the consequence is it creates an instability in the way you imagine a tennis match. Because the traditional view of a match is unstable, there is no continuity when you analyze your performance from match to match.

The error of judgment that comes from seeing error as random and chaotic also leads us to becoming an ISM (individual shot making) player. Continuity is the continuous and consistent existence of something over a period of time. Individual shot making is the reverse. When a player has an ISM approach, it creates a series of individual shots, judged as either good or bad. Over time an ISM approach will produce absolutely zero continuity between shots and points throughout a tennis match.

Competing as an ISM player will produce a chaotic interpretation of a match. Attempting to end points and hit winners will produce no stability between shots or points as well as between matches.

If we practice and rehearse individual shot-making on the practice court, this lack of cohesion will be transferred directly back to the match court when we compete again. This continuous cycle will be repeated tragically from practice court to match court and back again.

The second part of the argument looks at errors that are localized and stable, which means that we now know with great certainty *when* in a point they mostly occur. The majority of errors occur in the First Strike stage of a point (0-4 shots). Next, errors will accumulate in the Patterns of Play stage (5-8 shots). Lastly, errors occur in the Extended Rally stage of the point (+9 shots).

What we know now as a result of data analytics is that errors do not occur sporadically or randomly. From the data paradigm that has been accumulated by individuals and organizations world-wide at every level of play, you can overcome the illusion that a tennis match is chaotic and unpredictable. This enables you to diagnose errors properly and reduce misdiagnosis. The first step in overcoming the illusion is to learn to see error for what it is.

This perception of error as localized and stable brings us closer to reality. Once we grasp this reality, we will be able to think of matches in a realistic way. It is this accommodation with the reality of error that allows us to have a much better relationship with it. This relationship is more productive because it leads to stability and continuity.

The third part of the argument looks at how we can develop this new found stability and continuity. With a new conception of and relationship with error, we can grow our Competitive Intelligence with the language of First Strike.

The misdiagnosis of error

Viewed as random and chaotic, tennis matches are often seen as a battle of who's technique is last to collapse. Sometimes, the forehand never really gets started at all. We may dwell on our inability to make as many winners as our opponent. Noise and opinion abound in this situation, adding to the chaos of the match. Error is seen as free-floating and can inflict itself on players at the most crucial moments. The concept of free-floating error is important because it epitomizes the traditional mindset. Being free-floating also means we can fall prey to it at any moment. It is terrifying. Maybe we could describe it as an airborne disease that can strike us down at any point. This may be dramatic but it is this very quality of drama that makes error so diabolical in the traditional mindset.

If error is seen as free-floating, invasive and random, then it is being misdiagnosed. It is this particular misdiagnosis that causes problems. Below is an example of an identified error.

Identified Error

Traditional tennis culture will turn error into a disease that needs to be eradicated, a single thing that becomes medicalized. Focus, energy and attention are directed to this single source of error, the identified error. The practice court becomes a hospital where the error needs to be overcome[9]. In itself, this is not necessarily a problem. Technical glitches and collapse can be overcome. The problem with identified errors is twofold. First, it ignores or is not capable of understanding the nature of error in a tennis match. Second, and at a deeper level, it misunderstands and misinterprets a tennis match as chaotic and random. The second problem goes deeper and is the source of the first problem. Chaos and randomness lead to an infinite variation and contribute to the feeling of being lost for both player and coach.

Believing that you must master an infinite variation of options to play your best tennis is like opening Pandora's box. The idea that "anything can happen in a match" leads to an overwhelming feeling of lostness in the match. You may believe there are an infinite variety of shots available for you or your opponent to win the match. If you believe this, then you will tend to ignore the things that are relevant to your winning more points. You have your habits, tendencies and preferences. You will lean on your favorite patterns or shots when the match is on the line. Ultimately it comes down to the execution of your planned patterns, specifically two-shot sequences. Without a plan, individual and isolated shot-making becomes a catalyst for blaming your loss on technical shortcomings. This is the sickness of the traditional approach.[10]

---

9 One of the most common traditional ideas is to name our tennis training sessions *tennis clinics*. "Hey, I'm going to the tennis clinic today to fix my forehand!" This kind of language, borrowed from the medical industry, promotes a mindset that is grounded in eradicating error from your game like an illness in your body. This type of description will definitely hinder your ability to grow a competitive intelligence. Error can only be reduced by correctly identifying its main source.

10 See 'Discussion for Geeks'–Combinatorial Explosion.

A continuity of misdiagnosis

Because we are misdiagnosing, we are also misidentifying errors. Misdiagnosis works alongside our view of error and of a tennis match as random events. When the diagnosis mechanisms combine with our randomizing of tennis matches, we create this ability to find even more errors in our game.

This is an illusion creating the bigger problem that our new fake diagnostic tools lead us to start diagnosing all over the place. This gives rise to the further problem that we continue to do this and everyone seems to expect it of us.

This continuity of misdiagnosis is very unstable, prone to opinion and emotion. Instability makes continuity in winning points almost impossible. This is what drives us crazy about tennis and tennis matches. We carry around this misdiagnosis of error that makes the challenges we face much harder. Nothing really works for us and we rely on luck and the hope that free-floating error does not descend on us before our opponent.

What is the reality of error?

When you use data analytics, some interesting things become clear. The first is the way that error accumulates. The way that you experience errors when you are studying data analytics is distanced from the experience of the court and you see it in a different way. You can spot patterns and tendencies among errors. Because you are using a visual and numerical representation of error, it becomes easier to identify the habits of error, the way it seems to behave as an independent thing. This awareness of the flow and behavior of error allows you to become more precise in diagnosis and treatment.

Where does the Error occur?

When looking at the behavior and patterns of errors using data analytics, certain patterns repeat themselves. The first of those is the location and settlement of errors. We can see where the error is located on return of serves. This is the most common and frequently recurring location. We then refine or search by looking at the Deuce and the Ad courts. This will always give us another view on the location of return error as there will often be a difference of error on one side from the other.

For example, there may be twice as many return errors on the Deuce as on the Ad court. The difference in errors on the Deuce and Ad sides are rarely below 55 percent versus 45 percent so the player will make 55 percent return errors on the Deuce side and 45 percent on the Ad side. This is a 10 percent difference however it could more likely be 70 percent versus 30 percent, a difference of 40 percent. Whatever the case, you should look at return errors specifically separate as Deuce return errors or Ad return errors. One main reason for observing these Deuce and Ad errors independently is the visual cues of the angle of reception from the serve are dramatically different.

Another piece of data we can add here are the Forehand and Backhand errors, as the Forehand return on the Ad side is a different shot from the Forehand return on the Deuce side. The Forehand and Backhand returns should then be divided between Deuce and Ad so we can see where error is accumulating more accurately.[11]

How and Why

Identifying the two locations (Forehand or Backhand and Deuce or Ad) and then the specific moments of error allows you to address the why and the how in a more structured way. This reverses the traditional tennis culture approach to error. In traditional tennis culture, the why and the how are always approached first. As we have seen, technical delivery problems usually receive the blame, confirming the

11 Please note that you can actually see where the errors have accumulated when using data analytics. It's very difficult to do this on the tennis court when you are playing as you can have no written record of it. You can't rely on memory because you will remember those things that have an emotion or drama attached to them. Memories are encoded, see *Discussion for Geeks* – Encoded Specificity

chaotic/random view of the tennis match in action. The error is seen as free-floating and technical precisely because the how and the why are addressed first, before even considering the where or the when.

Where the error occurs helps us build a framework (in this case it is the first part of Strong Framing). Identify to which court the return error occurs, Deuce or Ad, then Forehand or Backhand, and it frames and locates the how and why. We have framed them with where. We can then look at another dimension as we detect and select them when using our Competitive Intelligence Report (CIR).

Now that we know where an error occurs in each point of the game, it further strong- frames our error detection.

When?

The question of when has two aspects to it. The first is: "When was the Error made *within* the point?" and the second: "When was it made *between* points?"

Within the point the First Strike error is the most important to us for the reasons we saw in the last chapter. When the player is Serving, we are investigating the S and the S1. When Returning we are exploring the R and R1. The question here is: "Did the error occur on the R, S1 or R1?"

The error between the points is related more to the decision making process regarding the First Strike sequence. In order to make a decision about how aggressive the first 2 shots should be and where to place them, the momentum score will be the deciding factor. There is a probability associated with winning consecutive points. Probabilities are not based on guessing, it is a reality that occurs as points are played one after another. The player will need to consider the momentum score before deciding how much risk to take when choosing their First Strike sequence. Otherwise, a player is failing to negotiate with the probability. When negotiating with the probability of winning the next point, shot location and shot selection is critically important.

1. The when is in relation to the Momentum Score, the score according to the previous point, has several steps to it. From a data analytics point of view, we want to see when the player has won two points in a row. We give the player a +1 if they won the previous point or a -1 if they lost the previous point. They then start the next point at either +1 or -1 or +2 or -2.
2. The point score in the game in relation to the momentum score is more complex. Let's say the game score is 30-15.
3. When combining this with the momentum score, the game score, 30-15 can be arrived at in several ways.
4. The first way is when the player won the first two points then lost the next. So the previous point score was 30–0. It has moved from 30–0 to 30–15 from when the last point was lost. So the momentum score is -1 and the game score is 30 -15. So in data analytics we would say (-1) 30–15.

   Reaching 30 -15 could happen another way. If the previous game score had been 15–0 then 15–15 and you won the next point to go 30–15, the momentum score is (+1) 30 -15.

Our objective here is to look at the interplay between game score and momentum score. We want to show that there is a level of precision when looking at the momentum and game score relationship that dramatically increases the chances of a successful diagnosis of the how and why.

Error will have several locations and settlements simultaneously

Using data analytics, we don't just find errors in returns. Most of the errors will be spread between three of the first four First Strike shots, R,

S1, R1.[12] Most of the errors will settle in the R but the other two will come a close second or third. Because we have the three shots together, we are able to see a more complete picture of the match and the location of errors.

Once the elements of data analytics are in place, we can reorder things and begin to detect errors.

The data analytics process then runs as follows:

1. Is the momentum score +1 or -1?
2. Identify the shot; R, S1 or R1
3. Deuce or Ad?
4. Identify the two-shot combination in terms of Forehand and Backhand on the return R and the R1:

   FH–BH BH–BH FH–FH BH–FH

5. Identify the two-shot combination on the Serve:

   3–FH 7–BH 5–FH

The more fluent you become, the easier it is to read the data and see where error is located. You can then make more precise and sophisticated error diagnoses.

Error and First Strike Sequences

As we become better at reading the data, we can add new elements to the quality of our error detection by allowing us to answer the how and why. One of these elements is the First Strike Pattern that was played. In chapter 2, we saw how the First Strike Pattern is the combination of S & S1 and R & R1 and adds another dimension to the question of where.

12 The S (Serve) is treated in a different way and is, surprisingly to some, not a location of error in the same way as the other three shots of the First Strike.

The Serve and Return First Strike Patterns have their own features and we analyze them separately.

The Serve Pattern–S & S1

The patterns on serve are S = 1 S1 = C So the pattern is described as "1 C"

Then you can have "7 A"

The serve patterns are divided into Deuce and Ad

Deuce pattern = "1 C"

Ad pattern = "7 A"

You can then add whether the S1 was a forehand or backhand

So "1 C FH"

Thinking in terms of the S/S1 pattern allows you to "Look up" at your opponent. Looking up means you are not looking at the flight of the ball as it leaves your racket. Neither are you focused solely on individual shots. The player that is looking up can see what kind of effect their S/S1 First Strike pattern has on the opponent. Does it disrupt the opponent or make them feel comfortable?

Instead of viewing the Serve as a technical entity in itself, see it as a two-part movement that helps set up the S1. It is highly productive to consider the Serve as relating to the S1. The Serve is defined and perceived in terms of the S1 that it produces. This is an important mindshift for the player preventing the narrow focus on the Serve as an individual shot. It is interesting to note that players can often think of their own Serve as inadequate when they think of it from just a technical perspective.

Technical thinking on the Serve is almost always negative and focuses on shortcomings. Players who focus on the Serve as a technically inadequate shot are constantly looking at what the shot lacks. They carry this into the match and overfocus on the Serve, which never improves and they lose too many points because of it.

Over focusing on the technical aspect of the Serve is the prime example of going ISM. In this state, there is very little chance to see our opponent clearly, let alone construct First Strike patterns that provoke them into error. First Strike patterns encourage competitive intelligence by redirecting our thoughts to create continuity of patterns throughout play.

The Return Patterns – R & R1

The patterns on Return are R = B R1 = C So the pattern is described as B–C

Then we can have B C

The Return patterns are divided into Deuce and Ad

Deuce patterns and Ad patterns are the same

We can then add whether the R & R1 were a Forehand or Backhand

So B C = FH FH

Thinking in terms of returning patterns has two positive effects. First, it forces the player to focus on the Return. Unlike the Serve, the Return is rarely seen as a unique shot that sets up the R1. This is in terms of the execution of the Return and the Return as part of a First Strike pattern. Instead of overfocus as with the Serve, we have underfocus on the Return.

The second effect is that it stabilizes the Return and the R1 sequence and allows the player to look directly at their opponent. In this way, it encourages an opponent-centric approach to Return First Strike patterns.

The Return is frequently rehearsed on the practice court in isolation and as an individual shot instead of as part of a two-shot sequence. Practicing the Return along with the R1 produces a sequenced mindshift which aids better observation of when and why errors occur within First Strike returning.

Practicing Returns and Serves in isolation creates the illusion that the Serve and Return need only to improve technically rather than tactically. They are rarely seen as set-up shots for the S1 and R1 and instead are practiced frequently as shots of consistency. Rehearsing two-shot sequences (S/S1 and R/R1) will lead a player to create stability between them and reduce errors in them.

Why we need Stability and Continuity

When playing a match, you are continually vulnerable to instability. You carry this vulnerability with you when you overfocus on the Serve and underfocus on the Return. The instability is caused by thinking about yourself and not our opponent. There is simply no room for your opponent when you are caught up in thinking about your performance of individual shots.

By turning your attention to your opponent and trying to provoke errors in their game, you begin to reduce your own. This is not just opinion, this can be observed and measured. By focusing on provoking errors you are actually doing something positive. You are being constructive. Provoking error is positive in that it is also stabilizing. There is an inherent stability when focusing your play to provoke errors instead of perfecting shots. This is why your opponent can be a stabilizing influence. This is one reason why embracing the closeness between you and your opponent is so important.

Contrast this with the focus on not making mistakes. Not making errors. This is essentially a negative thing. There is actually no such *thing* as not making an error. So you are literally focused on the impossible. When you are in this state your opponent disappears and is replaced by an illusion of a tennis player who is better than you. The illusion that they are also luckier than you. The illusion that they hit more winners and force you to make more errors. Again, all these illusions lead to a terrible instability.

In contrast, by focusing on provoking errors, your First Strike thinking makes a positive and dramatic shift. A player that is *provoking* errors is very different from a player that is preventing errors. One is stable, the other unstable. So we want your player to become a player of provocation rather than a player of prevention.

In terms of language, we move from a language of instability to a language of stability. You can see this when players talk about winners. When you talk about winners you are actually in the realm of ISM. You think that it is good shots that win the match. It is here that you find the menace of traditional tennis thinking and its addiction to technique. For our purposes, a continual focus on the good shot and the winner encourage a very unstable way of thinking.

Continuity and Capability

Becoming a player who provokes error rather than trying to prevent it creates stability. At the same time, the provocation encourages and creates continuity. However, stability doesn't guarantee continuity. What stability does guarantee is better results. The capability that comes with provoking errors from your opponent will simply prove to be better than ISM and the traditional, technical approach. Stability is sustained when a player continues to focus on what is relevant to winning a tennis match.

The ability to read the match in this way has dramatic consequences for the development of Competitive Intelligence. It is an antidote to the chaos and illusion of the match.

5

Momentum & Probability

What Links points together?

In traditional tennis each new point is a fresh start. You are told that you should forget the previous point and focus on the next. There is no connection to the previous point. Ideally, says traditional tennis, you should start each point afresh. This 'every point is a new dawn' approach is a fundamental part of traditional tennis. It is seen as positive and motivational. But it also appears as common sense and this is part of the problem. There is, unfortunately, a great instability in this approach.

The traditional approach to point management is that points are not linked together. There is only a perceived similarity between points. An example of this similarity is the way the performance of the forehand technique is perceived from point to point. Did the technique remain intact between points or did it break down?

This technical similarity between points is predominantly seen in terms of the technical breakdowns that may or may not occur from point to point.

This perception comes from the traditional thinking that technique is the main cause of winning and losing from point to point. For example, on one point, your technique was sound and on the next point your technique broke down.

Traditional tennis culture causes the problem with an over-emphasis of technique based training on the practice court to improve competitiveness.

In this chapter we will aim to do three things. First, we will look at a specific way to help you negotiate the perennial problem of closeness. Second, we will examine how the illusions of traditional tennis work and why you need to combat them with momentum and probability thinking. Third, we will show how to apply this on the practice court.

Momentum Scoring versus Traditional Game Score

In traditional tennis, it is supposed that you start afresh on each point. This approach to each new point may seem like common sense. It seems inherently optimistic. Whatever has happened on the previous point, the next point is a new one. To a certain extent this is true. A new point is about to start. You could try and train your mind to reset and to look at each point in the present moment, in the here and now. The here and now would not have a trace of the past in your thinking about the next point. This may sound like a great state of mind to be in but, it's going to lead to two drawbacks.

The first is that it is next to impossible. There is always going to be some of what we call legacy from previous games and points of the match. Trying to deny that the legacy exists from point to point is simply not going to produce the desired result.

Second, the legacy of the previous point will assert itself on the next point regardless of whether you try and start afresh. It's going to affect you whatever you do. What happened in the previous point is going to have an impact in some form on the next point. The key for you is to accept that there will be a legacy from the previous point. Once you accept that there will be a legacy, you can filter. You can consciously decide what information you take from the previous point to decide what to do on the next.

The two types of legacy

There are several things that you want to avoid as the legacy from the previous points. You want to avoid negativity, for example. Negative thinking has different characteristics and patterns.[13] At the same time, you don't want drama. Negativity and drama are not necessarily the same thing. You can have drama and be positive. Both most certainly will be fully charged with emotion which will cloud your judgment and inevitably affect your decisions. For the decision about the forthcoming point, you are particularly vulnerable if the legacy is emotionally charged, either positively or negatively.

As well as an emotionally charged legacy, you will carry a narrative about the game from one point to the next and this narrative is almost always a fiction. It is not the reality. Sadly, when you come to the next point afresh, you are carrying this fictional narrative with you. This narrative is based on illusion and will more than likely involve exaggerating your opponents' strengths and your own weaknesses.

Your perception is distorted by the illusion you make up in your own head. This perception consists of your opinions about how the match has progressed so far and how you believe it may end. When you are in this state of mind you think the probability of bad outcomes are higher than they actually are.

13 Please see *Parasitic Processing* in the Discussion for Geeks section for an example of negativity.

The second category of legacy is what we call Momentum. There is no illusion with Momentum, it simply recognizes what happened on the previous point. Either it was won or it was lost. If you won the previous point you are in a +1 Momentum position. If you lost the previous point, you are in a -1 position. This + and - position does not refer to a positive or negative situation. As you will see, -1 is actually a positive position. Our concern is not with positivity or with negativity when you filter the legacy. You want to know the position you are in. This is primarily because you want your decision on how to play the next point to be based on the probability of outcome. In order to do this you need to know what the probability of outcome is.

Judging probability in making a decision

Recognizing the Momentum, based on the outcome of the previous point, is highly stable, has continuity and is real because it is based on reality. This is in contrast to the instability of emotion-fueled legacy. For the player trained in Momentum, this recognition of the previous point consists of two further aspects and both are concerned with probability.

Probability Number 1

There is a dynamic to points that are played in a game and a dynamic that produces a particular outcome. Put simply, the first player to win two points in a row in the game has a more than 60% chance of winning the game.

This statistic has been derived from data that we have collected since 2011. It is not one that you will hear very often. Understanding it, however, has a dramatic and permanent effect on the way that you play tennis and improve. We need to look at this in more detail.

The player who wins two points in a row is said to have won a Momentum Point, our term at the Art of Winning. We created the term to distinguish winning or losing just one point versus winning or losing consecutive points in a tennis match.

This statistic is an average across all the matches that have been studied and from which data was obtained. The first player to win two points in a row in a game will win that game 60% of the time and lose 40% of the time. This is significant because of the 20% margin the player gains by winning two points in a row first. Here, you need to combine this with another statistic to explore their relationship a little further.

Probability Number 2

The second probability is that if you have won the previous point (+1), you have only a 40% chance of winning the next one.

These two statistics have huge implications for tennis players. Becoming conscious of it allows players to make better decisions about how to start the next point. The reason it is so powerful is that every tennis player plays in a particular way when they are at +1. They play as if they are at 60% to win the next point instead of 40%. If they are Serving, the player who is at +1 will go for a bigger, lower-margin first serve and usually miss. If they are returning they will aim for the more difficult side (A or D) sections of the court and miss. More points are won or lost, usually lost, because of what players do when they are +1 in the Momentum Score. This statistic is rarely ever discussed, probably because tennis culture is blind to it. [14]

How does the Momentum Score work?

The Momentum score is different from the Game score. We argue that the Momentum score is the real score in a tennis match. Excluding the first point, you will be either +1 or -1. This means that you will have lost the previous point or won the previous point. So at the game score of 15–0 as the Serve player, the momentum score will be +1. Immediately

14 It is important to understand that the 60% win rate probability for the first player to score a Momentum Point will occur regardless of whether the player is aware of momentum scoring or not.

this provides the link between points. If you go a little further into the game you will see the ebb and flow between the points.

Let's say I am 15–0 and +1 and I lose the next point. The score is 15–15 and -1. Let's say I lose the next point 15–30. The score is now 15–30 and -2. If I win the next point the score is 30–30 but is +1. If I win the next point the score is 40–30 and +2. If the score goes to Deuce I am at -1. If I get Advantage, I am on +1 and If I then win the game point, I am on +2.

The relevant thing from a legacy point of view, is not whether I score 1, 2 or 3. It is whether I am Plus + or Minus–.

Some important differences between Momentum scoring and the game score

There is no Equality

The first thing to note is that there is no equality in momentum scoring. There is equality, both implied and perceived, in the game score. So take 30–30. There are several routes to 30–30. For example, I could win the first two points when I am Serving and the score is 30–0. My opponent then wins the next two points to 30–30. Alternatively, the score could have gone 15–0, 15–15, 15–30 and 30–30. Whatever route is taken, the momentum score will always have a Plus + or a Minus–. The only time there is no Plus or Minus is at the very beginning of the game.

Deuce is not Equal

This has a significant impact on the way that you approach playing tennis. The whole of tennis culture accepts the score of Deuce as equality or as even. From a momentum point of view this is not the case. The score will be plus + or minus - at Deuce just as it is in every other point played. We will return to this later in the book.

Momentum scoring recognizes a legacy that is numerical and not emotional or distorted by illusion. Although it may be difficult for you to implement at first, momentum scoring allows you to move away from emotionally charged decision-making.

When you are thinking numerically, you are more in tune with reality and probability. For example, if the momentum score is–1 then you want to turn it into +1 on the next point. If you only focus on the game score, for example 15-30, you see you are behind and the probability is high that you won't win the next point. But when you factor in the Momentum Score 15-30 (-1), the reality is you have a 60% probability of winning the next point by being down -1 in Momentum.

What effect does thinking in terms of Momentum Probability have on the forthcoming point?

Tennis players are largely unaware of Momentum Probability. Since the introduction of data, we have been able to calculate probability and to bring that understanding to the match court. At the same time, the data brings to light what players are doing in relation to the score and the decisions that they make. Most decisions about what to do on the next point are made in contradiction to the momentum probability.

For example, the player who is 15–0 and +1 with a 40% chance of winning the next point will play as if they have a 60% chance of winning. The player reverses the momentum probability from 40% to 60% and makes a decision about the next point based on this.[15] The important thing to note here is that most players will make this miscalculation of probability on every point that they play.

This miscalculation will have a cumulative effect and it will probably result in an extra 5% of points being lost to the opponent. If I am aware of momentum probability, I won't give away 5% of points to my opponent. If I were giving 5% of my points to my opponent then they

15 The Player with a momentum score of -1 will also have a similar reversal in perspective. They will see their chance of winning the next point as being 40% rather than 60%.

would most likely give them back. If my opponent is also aware of momentum probability, then they will not give them back.

Of course, there is no guarantee that even if you know about momentum probability scoring, that you will win.

What you are doing is using momentum probability to negotiate your advantage.

You play according to the real probabilities; make better decisions, fewer errors in the First Strike area of the game (0–4 shots) and you force your opponent into errors. You also force them into more Patterns of Play (5–8) shots. Whatever happens, you increase your probability of winning the point by reducing errors from your side of the court.

Back to the Margin Problem and Closeness

In chapter 1, we looked at a fundamental misconception about tennis matches. That is, they are closer than you think. The game score deceives you and at the same time you find this closeness uncomfortable. So much so that you want to sprint to the finish line. You opt for sprinting over patience. The companion of the sprint is the dramatic or the spectacular. Players think they have to do more to win and this means they try low percentage "better" shots. This forces them into more error.

The problem for our player is that they cannot see this closeness. They can't feel it either, let alone understand it. The pressure of the match compounds this problem so you are unable to detect this margin. This is why we call it the *hidden margin.*

The margin is difficult to grasp or apprehend in a match. You become lost and look to individual shots and technical proficiency to bring you through. So this combination of great shots and fear of technique not breaking down acts as our guide between points. Sadly, this is all that most players have in their battle with closeness and it's not enough.

Momentum probability scoring is not going to stop the hidden margin being hidden. It is always going to be so, a perennial problem that's not going away and should be treated as such.

Momentum probability gives you a guide based on reality and not the illusion of ISM (Individual Shot Making) or the Game Score. Instead of an emotional or judgemental reaction based on illusion you have the recognition of reality and the stability of probability.

Thinking about numbers from point to point will allow you to calm down and select a better response to your opponent in the upcoming point. Your decisions about how to play the next point are directly related to the result of the last point you played. The momentum score is a guidepost towards making decisions based on the reality of probabilities instead of the deceptive perception of the inflated game score.

Stability, Continuity and Patience

Helping you move from point to point in a stable way allows for continuity and the development of patience. Each point has a purpose that can be defined numerically. You can carry this framework from point to point. Here is an illustration of how.

When you begin the game and you are the Serve player, decide before you play the first point on your S/S1 pattern. For example:

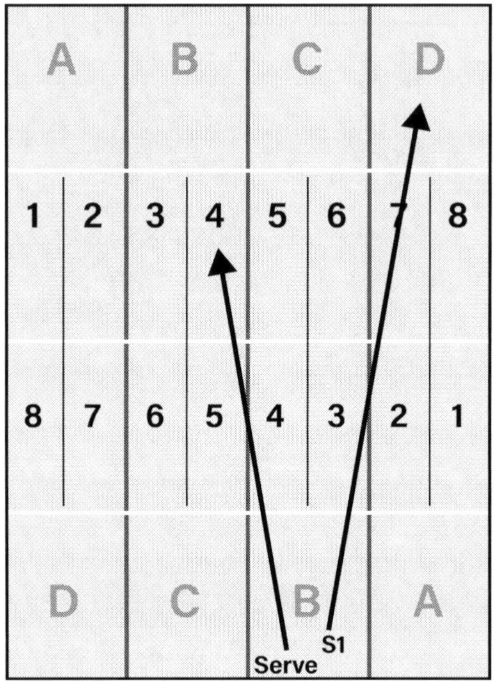

Now that you've chosen 4-D as your pattern. The diagram above shows the Return came back to your FH (Right-handed player) and you hit to D. If the Return happens to come back to your BH, the pattern would look like this:

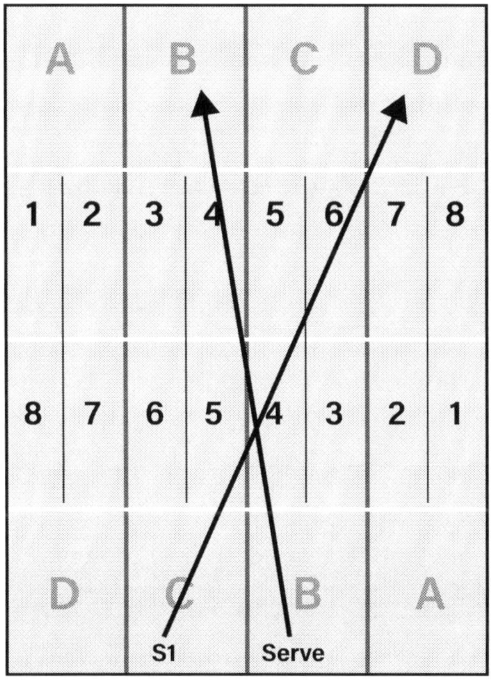

Whether you play a Forehand or Backhand after the Serve, you are committed to play the S1 shot to Zone D.

This is a highly stable way to approach a tennis match. It encourages better decision-making and it encourages patience. It allows you to Look Up at your opponent. Instead of focusing on ourselves and our precious technique, you can focus your attention towards your opponent. You can start to choose between two fundamentally different types of First Strike Patterns.

The First Strike patterns

When you are beginning the next point you have a decision to make. You have looked at which Momentum Probability +1 or -1 you are in. The question you want to answer now is: "What are my options and how are they framed?"

Let's begin with your opponent winning the first point of the game, you are then -1 Momentum score and it is 15–0 in the game score.[16] You know that if your opponent wins the next point and you go down to–2 (30-0), then they stand between 60–70% chance of winning the game. You also know that the probability of the player winning that next point and you going down to -2 (30-0) is 40%.

Because you are in a 40% position it is tempting to call this "defensive". The word defensive, however, causes several problems. There is no such thing as defensive in tennis. By using the term you can also encourage the idea of pushing the ball around with no purpose. Instead, we like to use the following phrase. Whenever we are in a -1 position, we should select a First Strike pattern that we think is our best. However, when we are in a +1 position we should select a First Strike pattern that we think our opponent *'likes the least'*.

What my opponent likes the least

When you look at the data from First Strike, you can see that certain patterns provoke an error from opponents more than others. Part of the capability you add to your tennis consciousness is spotting specifically what your opponent does not like. You will be able to gauge this by experimenting with different patterns.

This capability is fundamental to developing Competitive Intelligence. When it comes to First Strike patterns that our opponents like the least, there are clear options below.

16 The reason you are taking account of the game score here is because you want to illustrate the situation, not necessarily what the calculation of the player should be for the next point.

Here again is our court schema

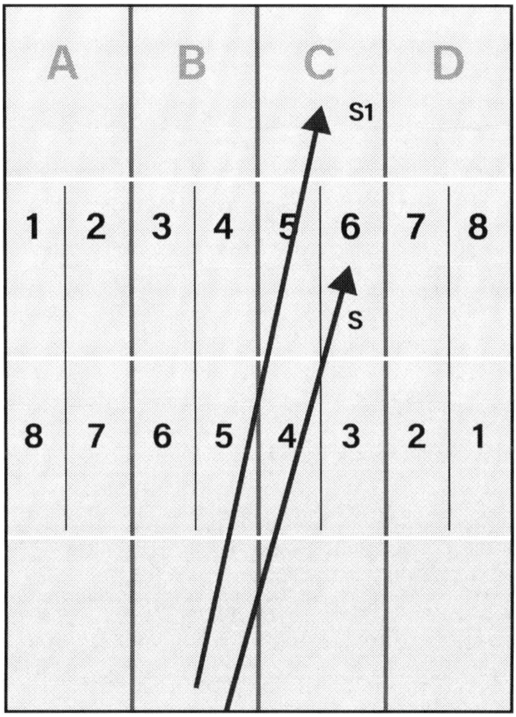

If the Serve player is +1 (15- 0), you know they will be serving from the Ad court. At +1, you are only at 40% and you need to create a high margin. This means that the Serve (S) should be directed into 6/7 and the S1 into B/C (in the above example into C).

This is an example of a strong First Strike pattern for +1 points on the Ad side for the server. The framework for your thinking should be the zones of the court with high margins, big shots to big targets. These are the central zones 2 / 3 and 6 / 7 on the Serve and B/C on the S1.

This is the framework for S and S1 for the +1 momentum score scenario. As you prioritize reducing your errors, this +1 framework will also be the most likely to provoke an error from your opponent. It is the First Strike Framework that has the highest probability of invoking error at some stage in the rally. You need this to negotiate with the hidden margin and move from point to point in a stable way.

What I am best at

The second fundamental First Strike pattern occurs when the score is–1 and 0–15 for the Server. You know that the probability for the player to win is going to be 60% for the next point. The 60% probability allows the Serve player to be more aggressive and direct to zones with less margin. So instead of playing to zones 6/7 then C, our player can play to 5/8 A or D. This is the pattern that the player is best at.

The obvious question here is: "How does the player know what they are best at?" They will know from the practice court, having completed *The Art of Winning Games*. Before you have done this, you will most likely hold an opinion about which First Strike pattern is your favorite. Here, though, you have to make a subtle distinction.

Data from the practice court or from your previous match will show your best percentage First Strike pattern. This may differ from your opinion of your favorite First Strike pattern. It's extremely important for you to know the difference between the most effective pattern and the one you prefer, if there is one.

What a player likes the best can be different from what a player is best at. But it might be the same, there is no contradiction. Just because both can coincide, does not mean that both will coincide. A player might like to target the 1 zone in the Deuce service box and then play their S1 to D, but they might not be the best at it. This can often be compounded by the fact that the player may think they should be good at the 1D pattern and therefore will go for it. [17]

---

17 It should be noted here that we recognize players will automatically do what they are better at. They will also like what they are better at. So there is a link between liking and being better.

This is why we have made this fundamental distinction a part of Competitive Intelligence. Without understanding the difference between the two different First Strike fundamentals you will always do what you think you are best at.

The best way to succeed is to play the best patterns according to the probabilities inherent in the momentum score. Looking up at your opponent and having a framework for invoking error is an antidote to always striving to do what you think you should or what you want to do without consideration. If you want to hit more winners with glorious shots, you need this antidote immediately.

Momentum, Probability and the Games

Introducing Momentum and Probability thinking is an essential step in developing Competitive Intelligence. It cannot happen, however, without playing matches. You will also need to cultivate other elements of Competitive Intelligence which you will discover by playing the Art of Winning Games. This needs to be done both on the match and practice court.

You must see how the match and the practice courts are parts of the same event. They become one and the same thing. Everything you do in either court encourages you to look up at your opponent and to think about what they like the least. What makes your opponent uncomfortable.

6

Let the Games Begin

This final chapter of Part 1 looks at The Games. The Games bring the match court to the practice court and the practice court to the match court. Traditional tennis has never managed to recreate the match court on the practice court. This failure has been the source of deep frustration for players looking to improve their results. The Games open up this two way relationship between the two arenas. So far, it has been incredibly productive. In every single instance where The Games have been introduced to a player, they have seen a significant improvement in their results.

In this chapter, we will introduce you to the concept of Shot Momentum. You will need to understand the way shot momentum is related to First Strike. We will then look at the battles that will be fought in the Arena of The Games. Finally we will look at the individual games themselves and how they work together. This will complete our look at the new concepts we have developed at the Art of Winning and allow us to progress to Part 2.

Shot Momentum

During a point, one player will gain the upper hand. The probability of that player going onto winning the point is higher. It can come from any shot, so it's usually one of the big first four in the First Strike segment. We call this gaining shot momentum. The interesting thing about shot momentum is that it can be structured, it can be framed. And for this reason, it can be rehearsed.

For the Art of Winning player, shot momentum begins with your S/S1 or R/R1 First Strike combination and pattern. This powerful sequence can have a monumental impact that can allow you to dictate and even dominate the point.

Shot momentum is the combination of two shots.

It begins in the First Strike segment of the point. This is important because you need to see Shot momentum as being a *two shot combination* rather than the result of a single shot. The traditional tennis approach sees the player who dominates the point as the one who plays a good shot first. Traditional tennis sees the domination of the point as the result of a *series of individual shots*.

As we have seen in previous chapters, this single shot approach is part of what we call individual shot making (ISM). When a player slips into this traditional single shot mode, we call it "Going ISM". ***Competitive Intelligence is the opposite of ISM.***

The Player that has Shot Momentum is the one who creates the potential to provoke a weak shot from their opponent with the combination of two shots.

An ace or a return winner is not Momentum. The point is over, so there is no momentum to be had. They are both winners. Winners are not shot momentum. Here is the first qualification. These are single shots rather than a pair. This is why the term ***shot momentum*** can tempt us into thinking about individual shots.

It is important to remember that shot momentum comes as a pair. It exists as part of a live rally exchange within the point. Finally, it is a potential. It raises the probability of producing a weak shot from the opponent. It is important to remember that shot momentum does not refer to the shot itself or any particular, individual shot.

What can happen when you gain Shot Momentum

When you are trying to conceptualize shot momentum you need to see how momentum can move within a point. Let's look at four possible scenarios and the consequences, when you hit a shot.

Scenario 1 – Your opponent will hit a winner

In this scenario, your dominant shot combination forces your opponent to reply with a big shot of their own and they make a winner. This hitting of a winner has several possible consequences for your opponent.

After having a dominant shot (or attempted winner) responded to with another dominant shot, you lose the point and you may become negative. When you become negative, you shy away from hitting more dominant shots, in the view that they are pointless.

This approach creates an illusion about your opponent. This illusion is based on your view of what our opponent can do. Your opponent becomes the source of an illusion.

A second consequence of this scenario with your opponent hitting a winner is that you could reply with more aggressive shots and go for winners of your own. You enter a sort of ISM arms race. The chances of this approach producing a positive outcome to the match, however, are limited mainly because it is unsustainable.

Scenario 2 – Your opponent makes an error and you win the point

Your opponent could lose the point directly from your momentum First Strike.

Scenario 3 – Your opponent responds with a weaker shot

In this scenario, my opponent may hit back a weaker shot. This is a shot that normally lands short and high. It also creates what in some circles is called an *"Opportunity shot"*. This result is the desired outcome for the Art of Winning Player.

You want to provoke this weaker shot as it's an opportunity for you. At the same time as being an opportunity, the weaker shot response keeps momentum with you and maintains a margin of safety.

When you receive this opportunity, you will want to produce another two shot combination and avoid the temptation of going ISM and try to hit a winner. Instead, allow instead of *forcing* one of your two shots in the sequence to *become* a winner! In this way you remain calm and play aggressive percentage tennis.

Scenario 4 – Your opponent may hit back a rally or challenge shot

A shot that seems to have purpose but has a big margin. This final type of response from our opponent is actually a type of dominant shot. It is different from the first type because it is not a direct winner, hence why I have called it a challenge shot. This is the type of shot that we want to be delivering to our opponent.

There is no clear distinction between the weaker shot of scenario 3 and the challenge shot of scenario 4. There is no clear moment where the challenge shot becomes a weaker shot. The reason we distinguish them is to get you thinking about your opponent and their responses and not just what you are doing. At the same time, the better you become at First Strike Sequences, your capacity grows and you will gain more shot momentum more often.

Provoking the Weaker response

Competitive Intelligence is built around Scenario 3 - where your opponent responds with a weaker shot. This is the goal of shot momentum. The advantage for you is that shot momentum is generated with high margin shots. You are hitting hard into big targets.

By trying to elicit a weaker shot rather than hit winners, you are provoking error from your opponent. You are practicing what we call "*Positive patience*" or "*High percentage aggressive tennis*".

This is a very different approach to the one encouraged by traditional tennis. Traditional tennis elevates winners. They are desirable and to be praised whenever they occur. At the Art of Winning, we sometimes shake our head when we see our players hit a low margin winner. When we do this, people look at us in a perplexed way. They cannot understand why we don't like to see this ISM approach dominate the players' thinking. Our approach is that the sequencing of 2 shots is the key to becoming more stable and consistent.

There is also a tendency to think we should be striving to do something dramatic all the time. We think we need to do something better or repeat our best shots. This attempted cloning of winners is a source of both error and instability for us. The growth of Competitive Intelligence helps us overcome this problem by allowing our thinking to focus on what is relevant at any given moment in the match.

Provocation and *The Games*

Provoking an error in your opponent by making them hit a weaker shot is the tactic that forms the key principle of *The Games*. This approach will set your thinking alight and energize it in a productive rather than a dramatic way. It also sets you on course to accomplish your goal of *looking up* at your opponent noticing their responding actions to yours.

By gaining shot momentum, you are looking to provoke your opponent into going ISM. This provocation has several effects on your opponent. The opponent will tend to overlook the crucial movement between the S/S1 and R/R1 shot sequence. The chain of movement that we discussed in Chapter 1 on First Strike is easily forgotten in a match. This forgetting is the result of players focusing on their own shots one at a time and going ISM. They believe that hitting better shots is what they should be doing. So they switch from thinking about their opponent to thinking about themselves.

This is exactly the state we want to provoke our opponent into. Rather than battering them with big shots and attempted winners on our own, we tempt them with our two shot patterns into the ISM mindset.

Here we reach an interesting place and one that is critical to Competitive Intelligence. As we have already examined, traditional tennis culture is predominantly focused on delaying or eliminating technical breakdown. From this perspective, the constant companion of technical breakdown prevention is the good shot. Traditional tennis culture recognizes the best and most desirable good shots are winners. The more winners that are hit, the more we delay technical breakdown. This is an ISM approach and has all the problems that go with it.

In ISM mode you are trapped. If you think that delaying technical breakdown is the main objective in a tennis match, then you will inevitably think that good shots are preventing technical breakdown. With this mindset, good shots are a kind of antidote to technical breakdown. Winners are like concentrated good shots. Technical breakdown seems very distant after a winner has been struck. After all, you can't hit a winner with poor technique, can you? Instinctively seeking winners, however, is ISM. ISM does create some winners but this only completes the destructive circle, our ISM–technical breakdown trap. But it gets worse.

Something that is never spoken of in traditional tennis is offsetting. It is like banking, where a debt is offset against an asset. The debt amount, however, can be offset against a much smaller asset amount. Winners and errors can work in a similar way in the player who has an ISM, technical, traditional mindset.

The ISM player who is seeking good shots will make more errors. At the same time, they will make some winners. Very often they will forgive themselves two errors for every winner. They are not doing this consciously. This is why it is so damaging. The more winners that are hit, the more the desire to clone and to hit more. Again, this is unconscious. It is unconscious because it is so ingrained in traditional tennis culture. It is ingrained in tennis culture because of the constant repetitive rehearsal of ISM on the practice court.

Try challenging this hitting winner mindset (actually an ISM mindset). It's almost impossible. From a traditional tennis point of view, a winner can forgive almost anything. Mainly because, in our player's mind, winners are what should be happening. A winner can forgive poor placement and poor positioning. It can write off previous error. It can (very temporarily) revive positive thinking. Worst and most destructive of all, it writes off future error.

Individual, single shots versus two shot sequencing

There is a subtle but major difference between the mindset that sees a point as a series of individual shots and one who sees the point as a series of two shot sequences. The first shot becomes the second and the second is born of the first. This intense connection of the shots in the two shot sequence is one of movement, it unites body and mind and allows for deep stability and continuity. The mind that is built on individual shots is one that lacks this unity. For stability and continuity, we have instead, drama and desire; or drama and hope. The player tries to clone their good shots. They will forgive several errors for a single winner. Instability and discontinuity reign supreme.

The two shot sequencing that starts (and quite often finishes) with First Strike has to be constructed. The influence of traditional tennis culture coaching is so strong and so embedded in the minds of players that two shot sequencing must be cultivated and rehearsed. Sadly, it will not develop naturally.

To be more specific, it needs an intervention at the beginning . This is a very important attitude to cultivate. This intervention and cultivation of First Strike also brings criticism. Developing Competitive Intelligence, as we'll see more of in Part 2, has been an individual battle with traditional tennis thinking. You will have to fight this battle. It is where traditional tennis culture has an advantage. It appears, at least for now, as the only game in town.

This is why *The Games* provide an arena for a different consciousness to grow and develop. For a long time tennis culture will continue to be in the technical and dramatic, ISM mode. When we are developing Competitive Intelligence, we need an intervention. It needs an intervention because it is novel. The two shot sequencing and Competitive Intelligence will not blossom forth unless it is first planted then tended to and cultivated. It needs shelter from the weather of traditional tennis culture. It needs a different soil.

When you are adopting 2-shot sequencing, you will have to accept the fact that you are developing an approach contrary to the traditional tennis culture way of thinking. We have to treat this as fact. There is no way around it. Traditional tennis culture has its own ideology that has built up over decades (nearly a century). Its perceptions and ideas may be questioned throughout this book because this ideology is the predominant way that players have perceived, conceived of and judged the game. This ideology has no room for any other.

At The Art of Winning, our goal is to propose a different kind of practice court that acts as a haven from traditional tennis culture. *The Games* provide this haven as an arena where players can experience for themselves the transformation needed to improve competitive intelligence.

In order to develop and flourish, players will need to increase this capacity to grow. The capacity for improvement begins with a practice court that has been reversed engineered to look and feel like the match court.

Welcome to this revolutionary practice court.

Welcome to *The Games*

The First Two Battles

Before we enter the arena of the games you will need to be prepared. We want to help prepare you for the arena. There are two battles that you will be fighting in the games arena and they occur simultaneously. You can contrast the instability (and often panic) of ISM with the player who creates stability when rehearsed in shot momentum. Those that experience this transformation never go back. It is a total transformation. We then grow and enhance the player in their new environment and with their new capabilities. Before this is achieved, however, two battles need to be fought. The arena for this battle is the practice court.

The First Battle is the one between the player and traditional tennis culture. The first move we make is to introduce players to the new language. Even with the best will in the world no player is going to come to you and start speaking the Language of First Strike. It has to be learned. The player has to be willing to do this. This is where the games provide the arena to then battle against traditional tennis thinking.

Before we look in detail at *The Games* themselves it is important to understand that as you understand shot momentum and First Strike you will be playing people who don't. You will start to see the contrast between you and your opponent.[18] This will surprise you and you will probably have more wins. You will not win every match yet the contrast will allow you to start breaking away from traditional tennis culture. As you break away from this culture, you will simultaneously experience a paradigm that will produce more wins over time.

As you progress and other people in your sphere start to develop Competitive Intelligence by playing the games, you will be rehearsing with players who are also learning the Language of First Strike and shot momentum. You will be playing The Games with them. This will help you in the battle with traditional tennis culture because you will be consciously seeing what it does to players and how it limits them. This First Battle will take time but it is a fascinating and deeply rewarding process.

The Second Battle that you face will be to obtain enough discipline and courage to keep stable movement and continuity within and between points. To develop Competitive Intelligence, and achieve growth, there will need to be change and there will need to be stability and continuity. This, in turn, requires method and application. It also requires that this is done over an extended period of time. The final ingredient is that it is measured.

Progress is measured over time to produce stability and continuity. This approach produces growth. This process requires a target. The size and nature of this target is constantly changing and there will be multiple targets at any one time. Some targets need to be immediate. For example

---

18 The first thing that players notice is the tendency of their opponent to go very early into the A & D sectors of the court.

our player targets 3–C. The act of hitting this target needs to be recognized (or acknowledged) and we do this in the form of a score. This then allows for measurement and continuity. It allows us to compare from the previous session and plan for the next by resting the target.

This discipline of targets and measurement allows for growth. It makes growth a conscious process over time. It is not good for the gardener to water his plants just once. Everyone can do something difficult or challenging once. This is however not discipline.

The development of Competitive Intelligence requires constant application and attention. This is the purpose of The Games. The Games are not arbitrary. They are not there simply because they are fun or provide vigorous exercise (both of which they do in more than ample supply).

The Games provide more than this. They provide an arena for growth. Providing an arena for growth, however, is not some vague term or cliche when it comes to the development of a tennis player. It is a commitment. With this commitment must come discipline. This discipline requires targets that are constantly assessed, reset and added to. This is exactly what The Games do.

The beauty of The Games Arena is that it is both flexible and innovative. The constant interplay of target setting and resetting with execution and the demands of the match court and interaction with data provide a rich environment for the growth of competitive intelligence. At the same time, it calls upon and helps grow the character of the player. The application of discipline cannot fail to grow the capacities of character. The more your character grows, the deeper and more profound the change can be. This concept of growth on the practice court with The Games Arena applies to all levels. Beginner to ATP tour, growth occurs in The Games Arena.

So what does this garden of Games look like? What is the climate and how do we cultivate? In the next section we will look at how the Arena is constructed by The Games.

The Games Arena – The practice court

Let's start by defining some terms. When we say The Games their real title is Competitive Intelligence Games. We give them this name because this is what we are trying to achieve with everything we do on the practice court. Everything we do at The Art of Winning is pitched to create Competitive Intelligence. This is why we combine what we are doing (the Games) with their purpose; Developing Competitive Intelligence. For the sake of brevity, I will shorten Competitive Intelligence Games to ***CIG***.

The Games have two constitutional parts. The first is that they all contain the Serve and Return. The second is that they are scored. All CIG contain points. The CIG are divided into Momentum Games and First Strike Games. Sometimes they are combined. Momentum games emphasize the movement between points, whilst First Strike games emphasize the movement within points. We will look at three games in more detail. One will be a First Strike game, one a Momentum and one First Strike with specific target zones.

First Strike Points

First Strike Games are played to 7 or 10 points. In this example we will use 7 points. The server keeps the serve until 7 points are reached.

The player can win 1 or 2 points.

If the player hits the first two shots into play, the S–S1 or the R–R1 then they receive a bonus point called a First Strike Point (FSP).

The player who wins the point will receive 1 point, the Winning Point (WP).

If an error is made on the Serve (a double fault), a single point is awarded to the returner. If an error is made on the Return, a single point is awarded to the server. The First Strike Point (bonus point) is not awarded as the first x2 shots have not been made. This is the beginning variation of the First Strike Point Game.

Variations

Play to 7 or 10 points

Play entire game from one side (Deuce or Ad)

If a Double Fault occurs, 2 points are awarded to the Return player. If a missed Return occurs, 2 points are awarded to the Serve player.

Deuces are Wild

The first player to win x2 consecutive points wins the game. The Momentum Score is never tied, you will either be +1 or -1. Serve rotates to the next player after a Momentum point is won (x2 consecutive points).

Training to gain shot momentum

The range of gaining shot momentum is large. For example, within a specified target range, the archer's arrow can land at several different places within the target area. The bullseye is still an area even though it is a smaller, defined area. It is not a point. So the arrow can land at several places within the bullseye range and so can any other arrow and still be counted as hitting the bullseye.

Our shot momentum works in a similar way

It is not a target unless it is targeted.

At first sight, nothing will strike you as any different. It's just tennis players playing in a group lesson. If you stop any player, however, and ask them what they are doing, they will reply in a strange language. It's

English but it sounds like mathematical code.

"I'm serving to Position 1 and my S1 is a forehand into C."

"What game are you playing?"

"SIRI"

English but you don't understand them. Not at first.

Part 2

7

Working with Players

In this chapter, we are going to look at four different types of players. Please skip to the one that applies to you but we advise reading at least two of them. Reading about the other categories will give you meaningful insights. These insights from the other categories will help you understand your relationship with your opponent.

The categories are paired. The beginner wants to become a good club player. The top junior wants to play on the ATP tour or US college level. The beginner may dream about being an ATP tour player; no problem with that. It will, however, stay as a dream.

The player that works with us will work on First Strike principles. The ATP tour player and the beginner will work on First Strike. They will work on it in a different way but this is the center of their work. This is what makes *The Art of Winning* tennis coaching great fun and so rewarding. We've tried to develop common, universal principles. We then apply these principles. First Strike is the most important. We continue to develop our dialogue with each of the categories of player using the language of First Strike.

The context for each player is different. Playing your first match or playing in the final of Wimbledon are two different contexts. Players have different resources. They have different goals. There are clear categories of players. These categories of players are based on the contexts in which they play.

No matter what your level of play, every player in the world is a First Strike player.

Every player's first goal of consistency is to master the First Strike shots. The First Strike shots can be offensive, defensive, or rally shots. Consistency begins with the First 2 Shots. All matches are decided by which player is more effective and consistent with the First Strike shots.

Here are the four categories of players.

The Club Player

The Beginner

Young Junior to top Junior

The ATP/WTA Tour Player

We'll look at each of these in turn below.

The Club Player

The club player benefits dramatically by adopting the language of First Strike. The biggest beneficiaries are playing the first 2 shots with higher margin First Strike patterns beginning with the serve into Positions 2,3 on the Deuce Court and Positions 5,6 on the Ad Court.

They then play the 2nd shot, the S1 into Zones B and C. Moving away from attacks on A and D will mean that the margin of shot is increased and there is a reduction of errors. The club player will want to begin focusing more on their movement between the two First Strike shots.

There is a movement flow that can be established through deliberate rehearsal between the S and S1 as well as the R and R1. As the club player begins moving better between the first 2 shots of the point, they also want to begin looking up towards their opponent to predict the next shot to them. This looking up and forward after the Serve or Return to see how the opponent moves to the ball helps the club player anticipate how they will move to receive the S1 or R1 shot.

When you are teaching First Strike to a club player you can see the changes happening quickly. The way they talk to you is different. The way they move is transformed. You are dealing with a new player.

The Club Player's First Battles

The battle with traditional tennis thinking is intense. More so than with any of the other categories. The players we work with will have an addiction to technical thinking; they prioritize it. This has consequences.

Sadly, many club players will avoid what we are suggesting in this book. We need to start and improve the quality of dialogue with our players. We need to better describe what is happening and the First Strike potential. We have to be honest and see that the club player's thinking is welded to Individual shot making and technique: and that they have another addiction.

The second addiction is to rallying. Most club players think that the more balls they hit the better they become. You can see it for yourself. The endless warm-up where the player is never ready. The player thinks that rallying is always a good thing; that it should always be done and should always be done first. This is where rallying addiction is most destructive; players replace matches with rallying. Pointless rallying takes up valuable match playing time.

The club player will battle two addictions and their improvement will be limited by how often they play. Nobody talks about this in traditional tennis culture. No one asks *"How often do you play matches?"* How often a player plays is the most important question when the club player wants to improve. Playing more matches is the best way to play better.

If a club player wants to improve, they need to play more than once a week. A good player should play two matches a week. What is holding most club players back from improving is not playing enough matches. If you are playing three times a week you are going to improve and then maintain a high position. At twice a week, you will be playing well and be able to maintain your current level or improve. At once a week, it's hit and miss, you could play well one week and not so well the next.

If you are going to play, make matches your priority. For the club player, rallying is a waste of time if your purpose is to win more matches. Get good at match play not rallying endlessly without purpose. We are going to encourage you to have an Art of Winning practice court. The Art of Winning practice court and the match court are the same. It is a world away from rallying and practicing technique. The Art of Winning Games are scored and all have a Serve and Return. When the practice court rehearsal begins to look and feel like the match court, it becomes increasingly difficult to distinguish between them.

The better the practice court rehearsal of play, the better the match court performance.

The meaning of a match

Overcoming the addictions inherited from traditional tennis culture is the first battle for the club player. Playing more matches is the next. The third is training the club player to gain some control over the meaning of the match.

In traditional tennis culture the meaning of a match is determined by someone other than the player. For example: the player may think this match is important because it means they will move up to the next division if they win; other people say that they want to come and watch the match; the coach says this will be a big win for you. In each case the meaning of the match is decided by someone else. The player will then dramatize and add color to the meaning that has been adopted.

Club players will impose meaning and dramatic purpose on a match. They raise the stakes of the match in this dramatic way. They do so in the hope that it gives them more determination and will power. By increasing the pressure the player is actually outsourcing the meaning of a match. Players will tell you that they have to win this next match or they will miss some important opportunity. At the same time, players will also warn of some dire consequences of losing the next match.

The meaning exercise in the 'Discussion for Geeks' chapter at the end of the book helps the player apply some choice over what the match means to them.

Players will see that fundamentally one match is the same as another. It involves an opponent who typically will be of a similar level trying to win over you. The match will be uncomfortably close, every game will be a momentum battle. This happens in every match that you play. Meaning will be attached before and after the match.[19]

The Dialogue

When we work with players, we start a conversation with them. We don't simply issue instructions and commands. The main topic of conversation with our players is based on First Strike and Momentum. We would go so far as to say that there is a language of First Strike. By talking to each

19 Meaning can be attached to the result; to the specifics of the way the match was played, or both

other, we can help the club players make significant improvements. The player begins to report back to us from matches in a much more meaningful way. The language of First Strike allows both coach and player to focus on what is relevant to improvement.

The dialogue with our players improves over time. This improvement occurs because our players are trained to study First Strike and Momentum Scoring. They become good at analyzing Data. The study will change in form, intensity and sophistication. It will, however, form a permanent and essential component in building Competitive intelligence.

Closeness

Being able to deal with closeness in a match is a powerful capability. This is why the dialogue is so powerful. At a certain point, you can actually feel the closeness help you grow. You start to feel stronger because you keep the tension. Keeping the tension just means that you are staying focused on how the relationship between you and your opponent is developing. You are not sitting back and relaxing in the moment of being ahead in the game. You are also avoiding the temptation of checking in and out of the match, you are remaining steady with your thoughts and emotions. You are doing this by focusing more on the Momentum Score rather than the Game Score.

The experience of closeness, the capacity to meet it head on at least twice a week and to negotiate with it, will allow you to be mentally strong and resilient. Players report a sense of calmness and one of 'flow'; as opposed to frustration and anxiety.

The closeness becomes exciting and it can be understood. Once you've studied the principles and put them into practice, playing tennis matches becomes a different experience. This mix of the cognitive and of physical movement and energy means that you can actually feel yourself becoming resilient.

Tennis is uniquely able to provide this mix of the cognitive and the physical when put under pressure. Hopefully, you'll want more of it.

Goals

Play again as soon as possible

We would like to make some observations about the goals of the club player. Going out and playing another match as soon as possible is a very good idea. We find players improve and 'keep the tension' when after a win or a loss they play another match within 48 hours. Sometimes the tension is lost and the player will 'rest on their laurels' after a win or 'lick their wounds' after a loss and they will do this for too long. Get out there and play another match as soon as you can. This is the best way to grow as a player.

The club player is going to get better the more they play. Playing more matches allows the player to develop a First Strike consciousness. They can then learn to understand how to embrace closeness.

First Strike Repertoire

Another goal is to develop more First Strike patterns. For example, if you've been playing the 1-A Serve pattern on Deuce. Then, begin rehearsing the 4-A Serve pattern. Players who expand their repertoire from strong foundational principles can only improve. The best way to implement First Strike Patterns is to define them on the practice court during rehearsal. For the club player this practice court is almost a magic place. The player gradually moves from reacting to the shots of their opponent, and going ISM, to creating patterns. This shift from being a reactive player who plays one shot at a time to a First Strike Pattern player is a powerful experience. This new tactical approach means that the club player becomes an opponent orientated player.

Over Focusing and Big Targets

When the player is developing their First Strike repertoire, they will face an interesting challenge. During rehearsals, the player will deliberately try and direct the ball to more specific target areas. For example, with good club players they will start to use the 1–8 target positions on the Serve followed by trying to hit the A,B,C,D zones with the S1 shot. Their First Strike combination could be something like 2–C or 7–A.

The R and R1 combinations become more targeted too; for example, C–C or C–A or even A–A. The target zones are there to focus your thoughts towards a specific area of the court. This is why rehearsal is so powerful.

Ideally, different First Strike patterns become more habitual and are performed with increasing ease. But the player should avoid overfocusing on the target. Players will want to play their shots to Big targets with a softer focus. In other words, attempt to hit your target without trying too hard. This means that in a match the process becomes more automated and more relaxed.

Technical goals?

Here is Principle number 9 from the 12 Principles of The Art of Winning.

Principle #9 The *Tactical* determines the *Technical*

This will be the biggest revelation for the club player who wants to improve. Every club player is preoccupied technically with their Serve, their Forehand or Backhand. Either one of these shots can ruin the player's life (or at least be seen as the biggest challenge to overcome). Even if the other two are going well, one will be demonized. In fact, the better the other two shots, the worse the offending shot is treated. To be more accurate, the offending single shot is often held completely responsible for the loss of the match. In this scenario, the bad shot is held responsible even if the other shots have been performing really well.

Tactical thinking provides a context for technical adjustments. Seeing this principle work day after day, brings it home to you how true it is. With tactical strong framing, the player makes accurate technical improvements faster. The player selects what is relevant to their situation based on their personal history. Having framed the problem in this historical way, the player can look at relevant tactical questions.

These tactical questions can be,

"What First Strike 2-shot pattern was I doing?" "Was it working?"

"Why was it not working?"

"What can I do about it right now?"

Examining these tactical questions will produce certain technical questions that will be relevant to the specific situation instead of overgeneralization the problem.

The Beginner

Please read this chapter even if you are a pro. Teaching beginners to become tennis players is almost a religious experience. Turning darkness into light. Reading about the genesis of a tennis player gives you a deeper insight into your own game.

As you may have already gathered, we love teaching beginners. When we have an inquiry from someone who wants lessons and says "I'm a beginner", we celebrate. Why? Because we know we're about to change their life. If that sounds dramatic, so be it; but that's what happens. Even if it is dramatic, they will be able to play a new sport. The biggest source of joy, however, is we get to play the magician or the prophet. You know they already have the skills to play a match. It's just that they don't know what to do.

The first illusion that beginners have about playing tennis is they believe they need to be able to do specific things very well before they can start playing a match. If we were to make a list of what beginners mistakenly think they need to do but don't, it would start with having good shots. Understandable, but wrong. Beginners think they should have the shots that good players have to start playing tennis. As we know, playing tennis requires no such thing.

The next illusion that beginners believe is that it will take a long time before they are ready to play matches. They think it will require a lot of lessons to start playing. Even worse, they think they may fail. Some even think they only have about a twenty five percent chance of 'success'.

Beginners need to understand that playing matches will make them better players–not that they have to be better players before playing matches.

The race

We know what's going to happen with every single beginner that we teach. We teach them to *be* tennis players. They need to acquire certain skills quickly, then they can start being a tennis player. It isn't a necessity to have all your strokes perfect before you play. You are playing or you are not playing.

Beginners need to start playing matches. Your job is to get them to quickly play a match. You can work on the technical details as needed based on play. There are three reasons for playing matches at the start. The first is that being able to play a match where before they could not is an achievement. Even if they struggle with everything else you teach them they will be able to play a match almost immediately. Second, scoring and the rules provide a system to learn how to play the game. Third, the match provides the framework for improving technical skills.

Teaching them how to play a match gives the beginner a tremendous boost of confidence. It increases trust with the coach. With beginners there is a hidden assumption: They think playing a match is not possible. By encouraging them to play a match, the player will become more aware of what they can improve for a more fulfilling experience. Their first lesson will be like magic because there will be a contextual plan to work through as player and coach.

Beginners believe they need to have specific shots before they start playing matches. We ask them what they think they need before they start playing a match. They all tell us they need a great Forehand, Backhand and Serve. We tell them they don't need these great shots to get started. They can begin immediately with very basic shots instead.

Most beginners do not know: the score; the rules; where to stand at the beginning of each new point. Everything they don't know is an opportunity to teach them–to build trust and confidence.

How to begin

In this section we are going to explain the experience of teaching the beginner from a coach's point of view. We are going to assume that there is one player being taught by one coach.[20] We like to start with a smaller court and compression balls, orange or green balls.

We make the court smaller by using cones and rubber lines. We often start with the service boxes as the court boundaries. They can progress to yellow balls as soon as they are regularly getting their first two shots in (S/S1 and R/R1: the First Strike sequence and combination).

It is important to start a dialogue with the beginner. Tell them they will be able to play a match in twenty minutes. This will come as a shock–and they won't believe you. Ask what they need to do to play a match: what they already know; what they believe is required.

Ask what they think is the most important shot. Most of the time they will tell you it is the Forehand. Tell them it is the Serve and Return of

20 In our experience beginners learn well in pairs. You automatically have someone with which they can play competitively. Where possible, we recommend teaching them in pairs.

Serve and explain why. Show them where to stand and Serve from the service line. Encourage them to track the bounce of the ball coming towards them, look for the spin after the bounce, and block the ball back like a volley.

Start with the Serve

Demonstrate a very basic push serve–with them standing next to you. They will soon reach a point of hitting fifty percent of serve attempts in. When they have reached 50 percent, get them to become the return player.

Beginners think that you should hit the ball low over the net. This leads them to hitting into the net when it could be avoided. When they block the ball on the return, have them aim between four to five feet over the net (one and a half to two meters). Make this the first target area. Players of all levels will aim for the ground on the other side of the court. We call this a 'ground target'. If a player aims for a ground target, they are more likely to hit the net. If the player aims for an air target, that is five feet above the net, they are less likely to hit the net. Note: Using a six foot pole, placing a cone over the top makes for a great visual air target for the player to aim.

Explain the major rules and start playing a match. Tell them how to score and which side to stand on at the beginning of each point.

Get them to block the ball on the return and on R1 or S1 after they serve.

Encourage them to call the score to each other before each point begins.

When the ball is out, players should call "Out" so that their opponent hears them. They could also signal with a raised hand in addition to the audible call.

Make sure they understand how to score the game and when the score becomes Deuce, how the game will end from there.

Young Junior to Top Junior Player

When coaching junior players, we first ask each player what their playing goals are? Do they want to play high school tennis? Do they want to play on the junior competitive tour? Are they interested in playing college tennis? Do they aspire to play on the ATP or WTA tour?

The next question that we ask is, "How much time are you willing to invest in pursuing your competitive level? At this point, we can now design and direct a practice plan to help players achieve their goal.

Obviously, the more time we have with a player for practice/rehearsal to develop their skills, the more time we can devote to technical and tactical expertise. Maturing as a top junior competitor will also mean that a player will need to compete at and above their current level. Players will also need to play a minimum of 2 to 3 matches per week to advance and improve Competitive Intelligence.

No matter what level of competitive play one wants to achieve, every junior player will need to develop their First Strike capacity. As we have proposed and explained thus far in this book, the first 2-shots of a point whether Serving or Returning is where a player begins their journey of consistent and accurate play.

Developing a 1st and 2nd Serve followed by a Forehand and Backhand S1 is critical to being able to hold Serve as often as possible.

Continuing with a high percentage 1st and 2nd Return followed by a Forehand and Backhand R1 is the key to breaking an opponent's Serve.

These First Strike combinations and patterns are the primary shots to master if a player wishes to become competitive at any level of junior competition.

There are certainly other shots to develop along a junior player's path, however no other 2-shot combination is more important to develop than the S/S1 and R/R1 First Strike Sequences. 60-70% of all match play points will end 4 shots or less, therefore the most valuable tennis strokes a junior player can develop are the First Strike shots (0-4).

ATP and WTA Tour Player

When coaching the Tour Player, less focus will be on the technical side with more emphasis on the strategic plans and tactical patterns. Many professional players have an instinct driven tactical and strategic plan. They have competed so often in their junior, college, and professional careers that their instincts are well-developed.

As good as instinct can be however, great decisions exponentially increase by deliberate pattern planning. This relevant data is based on current match play analytics and then deliberate rehearsal on the practice court. First Strike patterns have been emphasized by the tour coach and pro players more in the last 8 years (2016-2023) than the decades preceding. The main reason for this increased focus is the resurgence of data analytics at the professional level.

More players today are analyzing their data and beginning to develop better strategies when competing against rival competitors and up and coming new players on tour.

The men on the ATP Tour seem to be emphasizing the Serve and the S1, with special attention given to playing more Forehands after the Serve is hit.

The women on the WTA Tour in contrast seem to be focused on the Return and the R1 sequence.

Whether this is done on purpose or is something happening more organically is still a question to be answered with more complete data. The data on the one hand does show that the women on the WTA Tour seem to break serve more often than the men on the ATP Tour. The reason would be the men, on average, serve more aggressively than the women. The percentage of service breaks are less on the ATP Tour than the WTA.

Now, these statistics are beginning to adjust and fluctuate due to the increasing knowledge and recognition of these above examples. The men are emphasizing more precise Return games, beginning with better Return direction tactics on the 1st and 2nd Serves. The women are beginning to focus more on Serve placement, experimenting the mixing of spins on certain point scenarios as well as increasing the power potential on 1st Serves.

The great news about Tour players, both on the men's and women's side, is they are using data analytics to drill down and find the important shot combinations that have the most meaning in match play.

We, at the Art of Winning, use our customized mapping software to collect data analytics that are not yet found in most of the software presently being used on the Tour.

Because of our specialized analytics, we are able to offer a new perspective to Tour players when it comes to probability and pattern recognition using our Momentum Scoring System.

Styrling has worked with tour players using the Art of Winning Competitive Intelligence Report and this data has made a tremendous impact on those player's ability to plan strategic adjustments and increase their winning point percentages.

When working with Tour players, it's important to understand the data given to them must be relevant and tailored to their specific situations and goals. Knowing that they have good instincts already about their own game style and decision-making capabilities, it is critical to have conversations with them around what is relevant to the present moment in their career.

When it's all said and done, the Tour level players still play points that end 0-4 shots 70% of the time in match play. So just like the junior or college player, focusing on the decisions made around the first 2 shots of the point are most important. The physical movement between the 1st and 2nd shot is priority and that movement is based on the patterns a player decides to attempt as well as the response from their opponent.

Building a better game on the ATP or WTA Tours requires the player to master these First Strike combinations and patterns. Knowing how to navigate and manage the momentum score with the game score. Choosing patterns that best enhance a player's style of play and their opponent's shortcomings, within the First Strike phase of the point, is the ultimate advantage to win consistently on Tour.

8

The First Battles of Competitive Intelligence

Competitive Intelligence

In this chapter we want to share with you our experience of acquiring competitive intelligence. It has not been a straight path to enlightenment. Every day brings new insights and perspectives as we help players grow tactically competitive.

Competitive Intelligence is the ability to acquire as well as apply knowledge and skills with the strong desire to be as good as or better than others of a comparable level.

This book has been the result of five years of concentrated study of how tennis players become better competitors. When we began, we already had seven years of data (2011-2018) and we have been refining it and creating games and experimenting on the practice court since 2015.

The Games were created from a desire to help players discover average rally length and importance of the First 4 Shots. In addition and most importantly, how

to negotiate momentum shifts within the game and negotiate the probability of winning points consecutively.

Competitive intelligence is the ability to see, understand and develop what is relevant to winning. It can only function properly if the player is willing to explore the Data Analytics of their most recent competitive match play.

The role of data from recent match performances considerably increases the ability to recognize what is relevant to rehearse on the practice court. Reflecting on the data from the most recent performances and then creating a plan to rehearse shot patterns is how Competitive Intelligence grows.

Problem solving in competition

On a tennis court, players often seem to think that problems should go away and that, once they are free of them, they will be forever happy. We argue the reverse. A problem-free existence is a disaster because we need problems to grow Competitive Intelligence.

The bigger and more difficult these problems are, the stronger our Competitive Intelligence becomes. This runs full in the face of traditional tennis culture. There are those who want us to avoid anything difficult or unpleasant; happening to us or anyone else. To them, happiness is a problem-free state. Our approach is the opposite.

By using Competitive Intelligence, you have a completely different approach to problems. You won't reject or avoid them. You welcome them. Working with problems allows you to find *solutions.* Whether or not you find a solution right away, however, a stronger intelligence is being built.

We often say to players: "If you've got this particular problem, then you know you're in the right place." We encourage our players to want certain problems because this means that they are improving and getting stronger. Here's an example that occurs daily:

John is looking to increase his First Strike Capacity by adding a new serve pattern when serving to the AD Court. He thinks that he should be playing the serve to Position 8 (wide serve) in the AD Service box and then his S1 ground stroke into Zone D (8–D). His problem is twofold: How does he know if this is the right First Strike pattern to play and how does he do it (technically)?

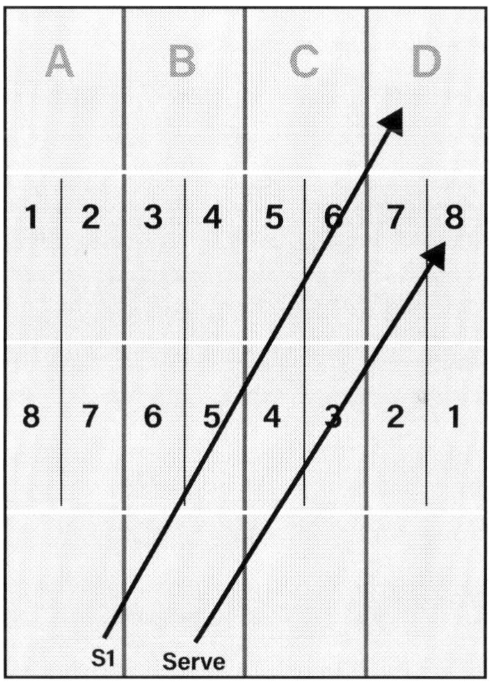

We look at this question every day, but before this problem, John could not speak the language of First Strike. We explored with him how to identify the First Strike sequences and patterns available. John was then able to decide which patterns to rehearse in practice. He now can begin to decide whether this Serve pattern will be successful against certain opponents, left-handed or right-handed.

Left-handed opponents may actually like this AD court Serve pattern (8–D) because John's Serve and S1 are going to be played into a lefty's Forehand on both shots. However, versus a right-handed player, this S/S1 Pattern of 8–D may produce frustration and anxiety because the two-shot pattern is played into the Backhand of a right-handed opponent both times.

Also, this pattern of 8–D will also definitely force John to play his Backhand on the S1 shot as most of his opponents will play their Return off a Serve from P8 back to Zone D. So, John will need to rehearse his Serve to P8 and then be prepared to play his Backhand out of his Zone D. For John, this may require him to sharpen his Backhand crosscourt back to the opponent's Zone D, since this is the pattern he's chosen to rehearse, 8-D.

If John's Serve to P8 produces a weaker Return to his court Zone C, he will be able to rehearse a Forehand S1 back to Zone D of his opponent.

To understand which patterns frustrate a particular opponent will depend on John's ability to play Forehands and/or Backhands from a particular zone of the court. John, now knowing how better to assess whether a pattern could be successful or not, has a positive approach. People think negatively about problems but a negative approach to problem-solving wastes the potential to build Competitive Intelligence.

See only what you want to see

Strategic dialogues with the player helps them move from point to point, to negotiate the pressure of the match. Every strategic discussion is based on First Strike Principles and First Strike Language. The better the player becomes, the more tactical options open up. For example, if our player is Returning, when receiving a serve on the Deuce court, they can try and direct the return into A. They then position themselves so that they hit into A again on the R1. So the First Strike pattern on the R/R1 sequence is A–A.

This R/R1 A–A sequence pattern can be rehearsed from the Deuce Court in practice during Competitive Intelligence games. The A–A pattern is a more advanced tactical variation of the R/R1 pattern B–C.

The B–C pattern on the R/R1 sequence from Deuce Court is a foundational First Strike tactic pattern of the returner's game. On the AD Court, this pattern can be reversed to C–B.

These two foundational patterns played on the R/R1 sequence to big targets through the middle section of the court are, in essence, crosscourt shots. The specific zone locations help a player focus for greater accuracy.

As a player rehearses the R/R1 sequenced patterns from Deuce and AD Courts, they will want to be aware of the shot combination of the R/R1 sequence. For example, let's visit again the A-A pattern from Deuce Court when Returning. This could be a FH-FH, BH-FH, FH-BH, or even BH-BH combination. These combinations could also be different types of shots like topspin, flat, slice, high and heavy loopy shots, etc. The type of strategy that is chosen will decide what type of shot to play with this A-A First Strike Return pattern.

The First Strike shot combinations are defined as the type of ground stroke available to play. Here are the four combinations for the R/R1 sequence:

FH/FH, FH/BH, BH/FH, BH/BH. If you Return and Volley the R/R1 sequence, then the R1 shot is either FH or BH volley, and perhaps could be a swing-drive volley, or overhead smash.

So let's look at an example of the First Strike language including the sequence, combination, and pattern. If a player is Returning from Deuce Court:

Sequence: R/R1
Combination: FH/BH
Pattern: B–D

Here's what it would look like on a court diagram:

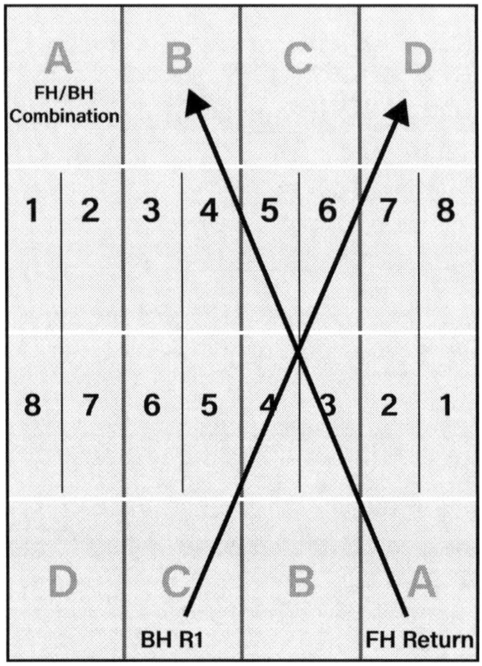

Once the First Strike Combination/Pattern is established, we can look at the technical considerations; shot selection, movement and swing path that will produce optimal accuracy and consistency. We start to break down the illusion that patterns and combinations happen randomly. We dispense with relying on guesswork and begin designing deliberate, intelligent patterns.

We begin to build a strategic plan of how to respond when our opponent Serves out wide and then plays the next shot to our Backhand (BH). Developing and rehearsing a specific combination pattern expands Competitive Intelligence within players.

By creating automatic responses against certain patterns from opponents, players develop patience and stability. They can respond more specifically to their opponents' shots instead of reacting in the moment with random choices.

Competitive intelligence helps us to see the difference between unlimited pattern options by our opponent to how the point develops with a ***limited*** number of pattern and combination options. We can use data and the language of First Strike to define those options available to us and our opponents, based on the skill levels of players in time.

Players will always face threats and dangers. These dangers are ignited by misunderstanding or overestimating their opponent's ability to play certain pattern combinations. Players will exaggerate their opponent's abilities under the pressure of a match, often rating them well above their own.

A greater focus on the technical intricacies of stroke production without contextual overlay is harmful.

Without context, the content of the shot (shot selection, swing path, and movement) can quickly become convoluted and replaced with subjective opinion. This kills off objective observation. It can produce an unhealthy obsession with technique. The tactical application of the shot will always determine the technical response of the shot.

Developing Competitive Intelligence vs. Traditional Practice Court Rituals

Disciplined patterns instead of individual shots

Traditional tennis culture values the player who demonstrates (normally visibly) high levels of motivation and determination. Motivation gives you the initial spark and determination allows you to carry on to a specific goal even if the motivation level has dropped. This combination of motivation and determination is classically called "Willpower" or just plain and simple "Will".[21]

Here, we are going to use the term *willpower* to include: motivation;

21 As in "The will to win"

determination and will.

In our experience, a certain amount of willpower is necessary to win a tennis match. Without some willpower, the player just ticks along, perhaps just enjoying the exercise or turning up because their parents told them they have to. Where willpower is lacking (particularly with juniors) then encouragement is a necessary ingredient.

Although some willpower is a necessary condition for a competitor to improve their performance–it is not a sufficient condition. We see many players, who start with plenty of willpower become frustrated with losses and a lack of progress. At the same time, we know players who think that willpower is enough to see them through a tough match. They often assume that the more willpower they have, the more difficult they are to beat.

Willpower needs organized thought to create an intention.

Willpower on its own is not thinking; willpower doesn't take into consideration your opponent. This is where a tactical context is needed.

Tactical thinking is thinking about your opponent. Tactical thinking is thinking how to provoke an error from your opponent while preventing them from doing the same to you.

The process of tactical thinking starts when a point has finished. Traditionally, the tactical context is one offered by the game score - 15 -0, 30–30 etc.

Competitive Intelligence, however, requires a different context. This is the context of the Momentum Score. The player needs to be aware of their position relative to their opponent in the momentum score. So the player will have won or lost the previous point. They will be +1 or -1. This gives them the probability score for winning the next point (80,60,40 or 20 percent). The player then assesses both their opponent's and their own First Strike patterns. They then decide which First Strike Pattern to deploy.

The decision on which First Strike pattern to deploy will be based primarily on the momentum position, the Momentum Score. Secondly, the player's preferred First Strike pattern or their opponent's least favorite

First Strike pattern most likely to provoke an error.

So our player is trying to provoke an error and limit the opponent's ability to do the same to them. This combination of willpower with tactical context creates an intention on each point and each 2-shot sequence. The tactical context allows for a decision to be made and an intention to be carried out.

As a player plays more matches, they have the opportunity to develop their intention with more precision. However, the execution of intention requires discipline. This disciplined, repeated and rehearsed intention, *2-shot sequenced patterns*, becomes a capability.

This capability is essential to developing Competitive Intelligence. You can start to see a marked difference in those with the capability of disciplined 2-shot sequenced patterns and those without it.

We as coaches will do everything to avoid the tactical. There are a couple of reasons why this may happen. The first is we overlook the tactical implications of winning because it is overshadowed by the obsession of creating spectacular shots individually one after another.

The second is that we would be held accountable for coaching players to take on more responsibility about their tactical decisions instead of permitting them to blame their error solely on technique so that we can now step forward and offer the solution.

The best coaches in the world rise to the occasion to teach tactical responsibility instead of technical perfection. The best players make the best decisions with the technique they possess already.

A tactically good player is far less dependent on technical coaching. The dependency loop of technique and repetition is broken when technique is practiced with contextual patterns. This new relationship between player and coach becomes a possibility when the tactical thinking becomes the primary focus of how to win matches more often.

When it comes to working with our players, we have looked to use willpower as an ingredient for Competitive Intelligence. What we have discovered, however, is that being determined is not enough on its own and can even get in the way of improving performance.

For example, the determined player, with a lot of willpower, often takes one hundred percent responsibility for their own errors. This can lead them to separate from their opponent by focusing on themselves. This separation pushes the opponent into the background of their thinking. You can see them becoming increasingly dramatic and often more emotional.

The more separated they become the more they turn inward on themselves. The more self absorbed they become. They start to think about great shot making (ISM); they inevitably compare their error ridden shots to their opponent's good shots. Sadly, this can lead to a disrespect for their opponent–who is at least fifty percent responsible for the win or loss of every point that is played.

Motivation and willpower become disciplined

Over time, the relationship between motivation and discipline changes. It stabilizes as the player improves because the more discipline the player acquires, the less they rely on self-motivation and willpower.

However, they still need willpower and motivation. As a player improves, motivation is internalized. Watching good players on Television could be described as external motivation; so could a desire for parental approval or impressing friends. As you get better, motivation is increasingly internalized.

There is less of a requirement for reward or approval. This is part of the transformation of the practice court as external goals and motivations become internalized. It is a fascinating and very rewarding process to observe in players.

Improvement

As competitive intelligence grows so does the capacity to work with error and closeness. The less experienced players or those at the beginning of their journey will have a big challenge in dealing with their errors as well as close, frustrating matches.

Players can become permanently stuck in traditional tennis thinking because they misinterpret errors. This is one of the tragedies of traditional tennis thinking, allowing players to continually interpret error as unforced.

Countless players look at error as something that could have been avoided. They should have done something better and will react to errors emotionally. Errors become dramatized.

With the growth of competitive intelligence, the player moves away from distorted and biased judgment (unforced error) and towards observing error with a more realistic approach. They may react emotionally or dramatically however the competitive intelligent player is able to quickly come back into the present moment.

Once this distance between biased judgment and realistic observation is established, then error becomes less dramatic and better decisions occur.

The time between points gives us the opportunity to distance ourselves from the emotions of the previous point. The space between points also allows a player to focus on what is relevant to the upcoming point. The player is able to reset their attention on the next point; specifically, the Momentum Score and First Strike pattern.

Art of Winning Principle 7: Winners do not win

There is a clear contrast between two types of player. The first type of player talks and thinks of the big shots that they must play to win. The second type of player is focused on what they can do to provoke an error by playing 2-shot sequenced patterns. The first player is focused on their own individual shots. The contrast between the two types of player is remarkably different.

Players that focus on their so-called unforced errors are self-absorbed and become obsessed with creating better shots. For the second type of player, the opponent is the context. They acquire skills in the context of how it affects their opponent instead of comparing themselves with their opponent.

The shift in mindset from individual shot making (ISM) to 2-shot sequenced patterns is the primary goal at the Art of Winning.

The players who are developing Competitive Intelligence are not obsessed with big shots because they are not relevant to winning. They don't allow big shots to dominate their thinking. These players do not think that they have to hit more winners than their opponents. Rather, they try to provoke an error. They don't have to match their opponent's winning shot with their own winning shot.

Developing Competitive Intelligence requires players to define improvement as tactical responses merging with technical skills. The type of improvement we are aiming for is transformational. It happens using data from the previous match, deciding what is relevant and rehearsing, and then go forward to the next match.

In the next chapter we look at specific strategic approaches towards this transformation.

We will look at what you need to do today to make immediate improvements.

9

What to do today

"I don't need long explanations, just tell me what to do", Based on that sentiment, here we go.

Choose your opponent as the context of each match.

During the match

1. **Slim Jim (Court Style)**
   Hit the ball into the Slim Jim Court on the first two shots. The Serve should be directed to the inside of the service box (Positions 3 & 4) on the Deuce court and towards the inside (Positions 5 & 6) on the Ad court. The S1 goes to B or C. The return shot should go to B or C and so does the R1.

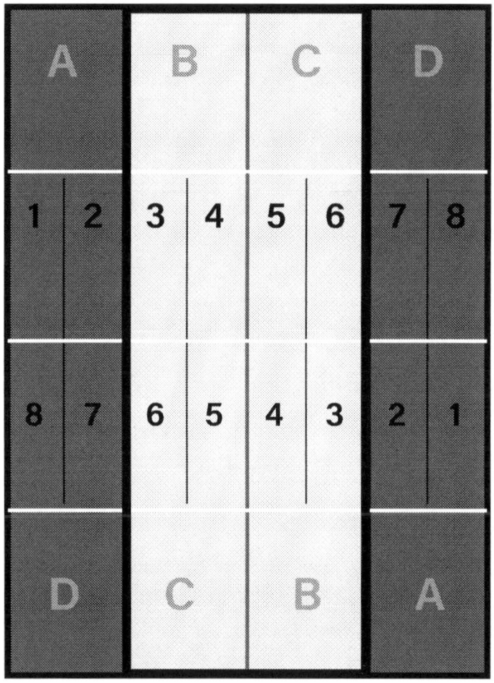

2. **Move Well (Movement)**
   Keep reminding yourself to move well after you Serve and Return. Your goal on the Serve and Return is to make a decision step (split step) in Zone B or C roughly three to five feet (1 to 1.5 metres) behind the baseline in preparation for the S1 and R1[22].

3. **Plus (+) or minus (-) one (Momentum Scoring)**
   Know if you are one point up or one point down before the beginning of every point (+1 or -1). Aim to prevent your opponent from getting two points in a row. Aim to be the first to get two points in a row. In order to win most games you will need to win two points in a row twice.

22 This is easier with the S1 because you have roughly half the distance to travel.

On the practice court

Stop rally practice immediately (maximum 10-15 minutes before beginning **The Games**)

Play Momentum Games:: Here is one shot momentum game and two point momentum games that we've created to get you started.

1. **First Strike Point Game**- set up the Slim Jim court style and play the points inside of this thinner space of Zone B and Zone C. You can either begin the point by Serving inside to either Zone B or C, or you can Serve to the outside to Zone A or D. Every shot after the Serve however is played inside of the Slim Jim court (Zone B or C). Each player will Serve the entire game until completion, play to 7 points and must win by a margin of 2 points. Once the game has been won or lost, the Serve switches to the next player and they will Serve the next entire game to completion. Each player can earn a First Strike Point when they successfully make their first 2 shots (S/S1 and R/R1) into the court, then play the point out until one of the players wins the point. If the point ends before each player makes their first two shots, then only the Winning Point is awarded. **Note**: The Serve player has an advantage because they can earn their First Strike Point and the Winning Point if the Return player makes an error on their R1 shot. The Serve player would earn 2 points, while the Return player would earn 0 points.

   A. Slim Jim Court Style

   B. Each player can earn a First Strike Point by making their first two shots in the Court. S/S1 and R/R1 Then, one of the players can also earn the Winning Point in addition to their First Strike Point.

   C. Each player Serves the entire game and then rotate serve when the game is complete.

D. Play the game to 7 points, must win by a margin of 2 points.

E. There are 3 additions you can add to the First Strike Point Game to make it more interesting and competitive.

1. Double Faults are worth 2 points to the Return player.
2. Missed Returns are worth 2 points to the Serve player.
3. Return Winners (Clean Winner–the Serve player does not touch the ball on their S1 shot) are worth 2 points to the Return player.

Once you play Slim Jim Court Style at least 4 games (each player Serves 2x), you can play full Singles Court (all Zones A,B,C,D). Play short sets to 4 games or full sets to 6 games. You can also alternate the Serve like a tiebreaker format for each of the games to 7 points.

2. **Double MO** – This game is a Point Momentum Game where a player must win 2 consecutive points 2x to win the game. A momentum point is when a player wins 2 consecutive points, in this game Double MO, a player must win 2 Momentum Points (not necessarily consecutively). So the challenge for each player is that the first player to win a Double MO wins 1 game. Play a short set to 4 games (you can win 4-3, unless you'd like to win by margin of 2 games) Play a regular set to 6 games, no tiebreaker, at 6-6, the player who wins the next game wins the set 7-6.

3. **Duck the Deuce** – This game challenges a player to sustain the momentum when ahead in the score. There are a couple of ways you can play this game. One player is the 'Duck the Deuce' player, this player once ahead in the game score cannot allow the other player to tie the score at Deuce. This means 30-30 or 40-40. If this happens, the 'Duck the Deuce' player loses the game.

For example, if the Serve player is the 'Duck the Deuce' player. The score becomes 30-15 in favor of the Serve player and the Return player wins the next point and brings the score to 30-30, the Serve player loses the game because they failed to Duck the Deuce! Same if the score was 40-30, and the Return player wins the next point and the game score becomes 40-40, the Serve player loses the game.

You can decide whether the Serve or the Return player is the 'Duck the Deuce' player. Only one player can be the 'Duck the Deuce' player during a game.

Now, if the non-Duck the Deuce player is behind in the score 15-30 and then wins the point to bring the score to 30-30, the game continues. Same at 30-40 becoming 40-40. ONLY the 'Duck the Deuce' player loses the game when leading in the game score and then allowing the non-Duck the Deuce player to tie the score at 30-30 or 40-40.

This game is very challenging for the Duck the Deuce player to sustain the momentum when leading and win the game without allowing their opponent to tie the score at Deuce. The non-Duck the Deuce player has a greater probability of winning the game because they have more opportunities. The negotiation of the momentum score within the game score becomes the focus for either player to capture and/ or sustain the momentum. Decisions on how to play the next point, the tactical patterns and avoiding ISM will be negotiated better if the player focuses on the momentum score from point to point.

Play short sets to 4 games or full sets to 6.

We have created many Momentum Games that focus a player on either shot or point momentum within a game. Check out our website to access **The Games** www.artofwinningtennis.com

The battle with traditional tennis thinking

You'll need to apply Slim Jim, Move Well and keep track of whether you are Plus or Minus one on every point, the Momentum Score. Your aim is to rehearse your patterns of play within the context of **The Games**.

From day one, you will be tempted with playing individual shots (ISM). If you play ISM you will forget to select the First Strike sequence pattern. At the same time you will forget good movement. Finally, you will judge your shot and not be in tune with your opponent.

By playing ISM, you will be responding emotionally to the previous point. Your decisions will be more reactive than proactive. When you are reactive, it means you are failing to predict as a result of ISM instead of looking up at your opponent.

Being proactive requires prediction, this can't happen when in an ISM play state. This is the main reason your movement reactions become slower from shot to shot. Your decision step (split-step) between shots is mis-timed and your reaction is late. Any immediate gains you make with ISM will be unsustainable.

Redefine the meaning of the match. Have some control over it. Use the meaning exercise in the *Discussion for Geeks*.

When you hit the ball, look at your opponent as you move.

What helps our players

Hit higher over the net: the ball will go deeper; your opponent won't be able to gain control of the point; you will have better margin and time to reset from your next shot.

Stop reacting to errors emotionally. Stabilize your approach to error by keeping your focus on 2-shot sequences.

Stop reacting to your opponent's winners emotionally, hitting winners is unsustainable because they are sporadic moments that will occur during a match.

Allow your great shots to become winners instead of trying to clone your winners.

Ask *"Am I forgiving myself for an error once I have hit a winner?"*

If you want to improve competitively, play more matches.

10

Discussion for Geeks

Contents

1. Facts and Features of Tennis Data Analytics

At the Art of Winning, we strive to discover and analyze the most relevant data in tennis. Our main goal with our players is to deliver the data analytics needed to become more competitively intelligent as well as elevate their overall match win percentage.

Since 2011, we continue to find in our analysis of match play the new data that enlightens and encourages our players to perform at higher levels of competition and achieve their potential.

When we first discovered the average rally lengths of competitive points, we built our competitive intelligence games, strategies and tactical pattern sequences around 2 consecutive shots. Therefore, our 2-shot sequences were born directly from this particular data analysis. If the average rally categories are 0-4, 5-8, and 9+ shots, then it only made common sense to us that players would build and rehearse 2-shot patterns to increase consistency in each section of a point.

As we have attempted to explain with great care in this book, tennis matches are won by the player who makes the least amount of errors. Hitting winners are great for TV highlights and especially for our egos, however they are not the deciding factor when it comes to winning consistently.

Building 2-shot sequences is the most effective way to battle the probabilities that are now clearly defined in the average rally length of competitive points.

What is fascinating to us at the Art of Winning is that just recently in the past few years neuroscientists have discovered that the present moment lasts 2.5 seconds. For decades tennis coaching has emphasized to players that staying in the present moment is the key to ***being in the zone***. In our first book, *7 On Court Strategies to Experience Your Play State*, we carefully described the Play State or Flow State and how to keep yourself in the zone as long as possible.When you are in a Flow State, you feel and perform at your very best.

Getting in the zone is a challenging endeavor, staying in the zone for a lengthy period of time is an even greater adventure. The mind must continually reset to the present moment subconsciously. The second you think you're in the zone is the second you are out of it. So, in order to be able to access a flow state, automatic responses have to be activated through deliberate rehearsal of tactical play.

We, at the Art of Winning, have discovered a system for players to access these automatic responses through rehearsal. Rehearsal is intentional practice, especially for a performance of some kind. For tennis, this means that your practice sessions should mirror very closely what is required in match play. The rehearsal is not just physical; it should also be a mental and emotional rehearsal of your match play performance.

Competition is the essence of match play, so therefore competition should be the identity of your practice court.

The practice court is the place to repeat your rehearsal over and over again, and the key is what you rehearse and repeat.

If the present moment lasts 2.5 seconds, then how many shots can a player hit in 2.5 seconds? You guessed it, 2 shots! It takes approximately 1 second for a ball to travel from your racquet to your opponent's racquet and then 1 second for a ball to travel back to your racquet. Give or take .5 seconds based on the speed variation of the shot played back and forth. This is the present moment, 2 consecutive shots for you.

In ***7 On Court Strategies***, we discussed the practice strategy of 1-2 Reset. This strategy helps you find your present moment, reset, get to the next present moment, reset, and then build a seamless strand of present moments. This is the Flow State, this is called ***being in the zone***.

The Art of Winning Data Analytics Team focuses our attention on these critical data analytics for all of our players and coaches. These include 2-shot sequencing and the Momentum Scoring System.

The Momentum Scoring System

Building and sustaining momentum in a tennis match is a difficult task for any player. Momentum can shift quickly back and forth between competitors. In order to manage these rapid momentum changes, it is helpful to understand how probability works. We have quantified momentum shifts in the form of winning or losing consecutive points.

The GPS Navigation System to win is based on winning 2 consecutive Games, 2 consecutive Points, and 2 consecutive Shots. We begin with Shot Momentum, build to Point Momentum, and then Game Momentum.

Winning 2 consecutive points and 2 consecutive games is the minimum margin you need to win. The first step to achieve this margin is to focus your energy on winning the shot momentum of the point, building 2 consecutive shots at a time, reset and repeat.

The Momentum Score keeps track of your probability of winning the next consecutive point. The only point that is 50/50 probability is the first point of the game (0-0) 0-0. After the first point the starting probability of winning the next point can be quantified.

WPP – Winning Probability Percentage
(1-0) 15-0. 40% WPP of winning the next point

(0-1) 0-15. 60% WPP of winning the next point

The starting Win Probability Percentage can be negotiated by the successful execution of how and where you play your First Strike Pattern and Combination, the first 2-shots of the point. The shot momentum builds to the Patterns of Play stage of the point (5-8 shot rally section). Once you get into the 9+ rally section of the point, the WPP shifts back to 50/50 for each player. This is the only other time than the first point of the game where the WPP shifts to 50/50. So, the real advantage and disadvantage of Win Probability Percentage takes place inside the First 4 Shots you play in the point!

Playing aggressive high percentage tennis on the First 4 Shots, targeting and pattern development is critical to negotiate your WPP. This is why rehearsal of First Strike and Patterns of Play stages in practice using momentum scoring can be so beneficial when you play a competitive match.

Win Probability Percentages using Momentum Scoring:
As we stated earlier in Chapter 5, there is a Win Probability Percentage (WPP) assigned to each Momentum Score within a game. Momentum scoring tracks the number of consecutive points you have won or lost as a player. The Art of Winning Momentum Score resets to 0-0 after a maximum of 3 consecutive points are won or lost. The first reason for this is to track momentum in terms of how many consecutive points are ***relevant*** to winning a game in tennis. Once a game is won or lost, the Momentum Score resets back to 0-0 for the 1st point of the next game. The second reason is the Art of Winning System has defined the Momentum Scores specifically with language to better define and track how a player is winning and losing individual points and games.

0-0

Every game begins with the Momentum Score at 0-0. Each player is competing to win the 1st point of the game. When the Momentum Score is 0-0, each player begins with a 50% probability of winning the 1st point of the game.

1-0 (+1) or 0-1 (-1)
When a player wins or loses 1 point, we call this a ***Direction Point***. The

reason is because a player is now moving in the direction of gaining or losing point momentum.

Winning a Direction Point shifts the WPP from (0-0) 50% to (1-0) 40%

The player has a 40% WPP of winning the next point.

Losing a Direction Point shifts the WPP from (0-0) 50% to (0-1) 60%

The player has a 60% WPP of winning the next point.

Each player begins with a WPP, and their WPP is based on winning or losing the last point.

2-0 (+2) or 0-2 (-2)

When a player wins or loses 2 consecutive points, we call this a ***Momentum Point***. When a player wins a Momentum Point, we say that they are creating *enough* margin to gain the momentum of the game. They have also placed themselves in a favorable position of increased probability of winning the game as well. At the same time, however, the player has also decreased their WPP for the next consecutive point.

When a player loses a Momentum Point, they are in a position where their WPP increases for the next point played.

Winning a Momentum Point shifts the WPP from (1-0) 40% to (2-0) 30%

The player has a 30% WPP of winning the next point.

Losing a Momentum Point shifts the WPP from (0-1) 60% to (0-2) 70%

The player has a 70% WPP of winning the next point.

Once again, each player begins with an increased or decreased WPP for the next point.

3-0 (+3) or 0-3 (-3)
When a player wins or loses 3 consecutive points, we call this a ***Conversion Point***. When a player wins a Conversion Point, they have created enough margin to have a high probability of winning the game. The WPP also shifts simultaneouly to favor the player who has lost the Conversion Point.

Winning a Conversion Point shifts the WPP from (2-0) 30% to (3-0) 20%

The player has a 20% WPP of winning the next point.

Losing a Converison Point shifts the WPP from (0-2) 70% to (0-3) 80%

The player has a 80% WPP of winning the next point.

Direction Point (+1 or -1)
Momentum Point (+2 or -2)
Conversion Point (+3 or -3)

Conclusion
Over a period of 12 years at the Art of Winning, we have discovered trends within the Data Analytics of Momentum Scoring. The first trend is that as a competitive player wins consecutive points their confidence rises and yet their concentration falls. As a competitive player loses consecutive points their confidence falls and yet their concentration rises. So our conclusion is that confidence and concentration flow in opposite directions. When one falls, the other rises and vice versa.

The Win Probability Percentage is based upon the psychological response to winning and losing consecutive points, the rise and fall of confidence and concentration. The WPP is also based on the trends in the Data itself, the numerical odds of winning and losing 2 or 3 points consecutively.

The WPP is a starting probability and can be negotiated by each player to raise or lower the chance of winning the next point. This negotiation involves first and foremost a player's decisions on the First 2 Shots of the next point. The First Strike Sequence. After the first 2 shots are played, then the probability of winning or losing the point shifts to the decisions on the next 2 shots in the point played by the player, the Pattern of Play Sequence.

It's important to note that the WPP is affected greater within the First Strike (0-4 shots) and Patterns of Play (5-8) stages of the point than in the Extended Rally stage (9+ shots). Once a point reaches the Extended Rally stage, then the probability of winning the point falls back to 50/50 chance for each player to win the point.

The Momentum Scoring System was developed to assist players in negotiating their WPP at the beginning of each point based on their current momentum score position. From there, each player can decide for themselves how much risk to manage in attempting to win the next consecutive point. Our experience is that this system accelerates competitive intelligence more vigorously in the player for the most competitive environments.

2. The 12 principles of the Art of Winning

1. 70-20-10 is top down ATP to club
2. Players play better when they are behind in the score
3. The Second most important person on court is you
4. Know Your best *First Strike* pattern and know what your opponent likes least
5. The *Momentum Score* is the real score
6. Become the House with 55%
7. 'Winners' do not win
8. You can't *improve* when you don't know what the real problem is
9. The *Tactical* determines the *Technical*
10. Perception is distorted by the emotional response to a situation

based on current beliefs.

11. A player is born with everything needed to win
12. Embrace uncertainty

Top 2

1. Win 55% of the points to become 'The House' and win 99% of your matches

2. The *Momentum Score* is the real score

6 Categories of Problem for players

1. I keep losing to "that" player
2. Over-respect (perception is distorted, I need to do more)
3. Anxiety (nervous)–think about yourself before your opponent
4. I play so badly (expectation is unrealistic)
5. I can't win
6. I'm not fit enough (I haven't been playing enough, I haven't been playing with the right people, I can't play singles, I don't have enough time)

Universal & Particular
Particular Training Mindset versus (Universal Training Mindset)

1. Technique vs Tactical
2. Mental Toughness/Emotional -Psychology/Personality vs Reason/ Character
3. Playing style vs First Strike Patterns
4. Fitness and Movement vs Athleticism
5. Winning every point you can vs Becoming the House (established patterns to B/C)
6. Rallying and Repetition vs First Strike and Improvisation
7. Hitting Winners / Finish the Point vs. 2-Shot Sequenced Patterns

8. Quantitative / More vs Qualitative–(Deliberate,Intentional)
9. Software vs Universal Operating System

3. The benefits of creating the opportunity to hit a forehand on the S1 and R1

The First Strike Forehand

The Forehand is considered the most important shot in tennis. Much of tennis coaching focuses on the importance of the Forehand groundstroke. In fact, 99% of the time, the Forehand is the first tennis shot you learn when beginning to play tennis.

Notwithstanding the two most critical shots in tennis, the Serve and Return, the Forehand is arguably the most important shot you can possess in your tennis game. So now the question is, ***which*** Forehand is the most important?

At the Art of Winning, we prioritize shots based on when they happen within a point and how often they occur in a match. The first opportunity to hit a Forehand groundstroke is the S1 or the R1. The language of First Strike is critical here and it means the first Forehand either after the Serve or after the Return, the ***First Strike Forehand***.

This First Strike Forehand is typically a groundstroke played behind or just in front of the baseline. As we have emphasized earlier in this book, your movement to position yourself to hit this Forehand makes all the difference in how effective your offensive or defensive response will be in the rally.

The most critical thing you will discover about attempting a First Strike Forehand is how quickly you should respond after the Serve or Return. The direction you move after your Serve/Return is even more meaningful than any other movement to any other shot you play in the point. You will also hit the First Strike Combination more often in a match than any other shot combination or sequence of shots.

Serving from the Advantage court and serving from the Deuce court present two distinct challenges when trying to hit a S1 forehand. You need to pay particular attention to the difference between the two situations. For example, the directional angle of the incoming Return to your S1 Forehand will affect your movement in a distinct way. This movement must be rehearsed in practice to be able to play more First Strike Forehands in match play.

One advantage of playing a Forehand after your Serve is that you will play your most powerful groundstroke at the beginning of the point. Your ability to create offensive momentum from the start of the point will become a big advantage for you. The probability of winning more points increases dramatically when playing a S1 Forehand.

The key to playing a powerful S1 Forehand is determined by the placement of your Serve. This is why you will want to rehearse **ALL** of the S/S1 First Strike Patterns from Deuce and Ad Courts in practice. (See below a list of the First Strike Forehand patterns)

You will discover the patterns you like best. Most importantly, you will discover the patterns that produce the highest winning %. In order to discover the highest winning % when playing a First Strike Forehand, you will need to play points that begin with specific S/S1 First Strike pattern sequences. For example, from the Deuce Court play 10 points beginning the point with the pattern 1-A. Play out the point and see how many times you win of 10 points rehearsing that particular pattern of 1-A. Then, choose another pattern and repeat the process. First, you will discover how accurate you are with your Serve Position 1 and then second, how well you reset to get yourself in the best stance and loading position to hit your S1 to Zone A.

When Returning your opponent's Serve, you are hunting for R1 Forehands.

The probability of winning more points when Returning is increased when a R1 Forehand is played vs. a Backhand R1.

The odds of playing a First Strike Forehand after your Return will depend on where your Return lands vs. the Serve player. It will equally depend on how well you move from the Return and where you position yourself to receive your opponent's S1 shot.

The R/R1 combinations should be rehearsed in practice more often to develop this specific movement sequence. It is essential to rehearse from both Advantage and Deuce courts. Moving left after the Deuce Return of Serve will be a significantly different movement sequence than moving right, after the Advantage court Return of Serve.

There are 4 R/R1 groundstroke combinations and they all should be rehearsed to find your favorite and highest win % combination. The FH/FH combination will most likely be your best. As with the Serve First Strike Forehands, rehearse 10 points as the Return player with a FH/FH combination. First, from Deuce Court and second, from the Ad Court. Record how many points out of 10 played that you are able to win.

At the Art of Winning website we have a First Strike Movement Series that dives deeper into the practice rehearsal of these First Strike Forehands for the Serve and Return. Check it out here: www.artofwinningtennis.com

Serve/First Strike Forehand S1

The Serve Positions and S1 Zone Targets will depend on what kind of Serve you play into the Serve Positions. There are 3 types of Serves: Flat, Kick, Slice

These are suggested Serve types/S1 targets for a player to rehearse.

Deuce Court

Types of Serve/Position	S1 Forehand Zone	# of Combinations
Slice/Flat to P1	A, B, C, D	4
Flat/Kick to P2	A, B, C, D	4
Slice/Flat/Kick to P3	A, B C, D	4
Slice/Flat/Kick to P4	A, B, C, D	4

AD Court

Types of Serve/Position	S1 Forehand Zone	# of Combinations
Slice/Flat to P5	A, B, C, D	4
Flat/Kick to P6	A, B, C, D	4
Slice/Flat/Kick to P7	A, B C, D	4
Slice/Flat/Kick to P8	A, B, C, D	4

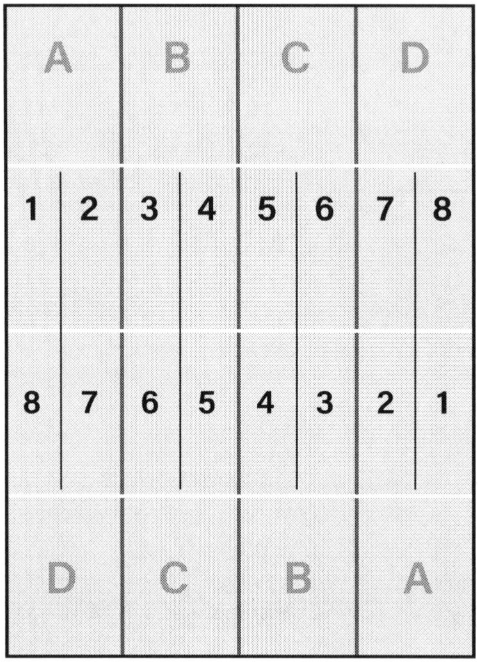

4. The Player

"I did everything you said, my backhand was much better in the match but I still lost."
"I'm not winning yet but my forehand has been much better in matches"

My experience of 'the loop'

When players say they want to 'improve' I used to be very quick to leap in and tell them what to do. Try this system; "You have to improve this shot and you have to do it this way". Looking back at my younger self, I can see that I was often not helping people at all and the problem was that they believed me. So what was it I was telling them? I was almost trying to compete with them over what their problem was and what it was they needed to overcome. *"You do realize that it's your foot position on the backhand and not your mid court forehand?"*

There was one thing that I remember about this so-called 'advice'. It was an attempt to impress people rather than a genuine attempt to help them with their game. Again, they believed me. Sometimes I would get resistance; like a groan or confused surprise. When I would tell them that particular week that their problem was *"Your footwork on the backhand"* they would sigh, saying that *"Last week it was the first serve"*. Forever chopping and changing, I blindly continued advising my players to do this or that and change it from one week to the next.

It didn't really get results. Sure my players may have looked better. My players were eternally grateful for all these new insights I was sharing with them (and they were paying for). Perhaps most tragically, people were apologising for not implementing the brilliant things I was teaching them in practice. I really could do no wrong. So we were mirroring each other. Endlessly. I can see now that there was no growth in this relationship. Taking all the glory and praise for someone's improvement and none of the criticism when it goes wrong is not a good place to be in. It is, however, very seductive. All the benefits but with no downside. It is a place of 'no error'.

And there was no *revelation* either. No road to Damascus moment. No happy ending or moment of insight. It went on for decades. It was never 'my fault'. My players would continue to castigate themselves and apologise for not applying what I had told them over the years. There were celebrations when something nearly succeeded. They would simply have to try harder next time. I was an 'outcome' coach. More than that, I was a technical outcome coach.

The 'outcome' was judged in relation to the perceived role the particular shot played in the winning or losing of the match.

Sometimes the shot was wholly responsible for the win, sometimes for the loss. Often, the shot had begun to work but ultimately let the player down. In any case, it was never my fault and always required more work on the part of my player.

When I changed careers, I experienced the consequences of this 'protected outcome' dynamic in a dramatic and frightening fashion. At first it was business as usual for me. There was a little excitement from my employers and their clients about what I could produce. I had become used to making people feel good about themselves regardless of outcome. This worked initially and I was praised and had a little 'guru' status for a while. This, however, was temporary. The field I had chosen explicitly required an acknowledgement of the results. There was no shielded outcome, no deflected blame where the customer took responsibility for the result that I had a part in creating. There was little praise for a good outcome either as it was seen as the result of something other than my great work. After a time the 'shielded outcome' started to disintegrate and go into reverse.

I was being doubted and questioned for a lack of results. I was not used to this. My ego said I should only work with people who thought I was great. After all, this was what I had created for myself in tennis. I wasn't terrible at what I was doing, I did get some good outcomes. It was simply that the results some people wanted were not forthcoming. I wasn't able to handle this. I was 'hard wired' to think it was their fault and never mine.

Thankfully, I fell back in with the right crowd. It came from learning that 70% of points in tennis are over before the 5th shot is played. It may not sound like much but that was the moment I credit for the onset of real change.

What does *improvement* actually mean?

When I speak with players they want to know how to get better, they want to 'improve'. Now this word 'improve' seems fairly straightforward. I want to make an 'improvement'. I want to become better at something.

When people say that they want to 'improve' they seem to bring two assumptions or two pre-conditions to the table. First, people attempt to ***identify*** what needs to be improved and what they may need ***to acquire*** (to have). Second, people identify how they are going to go about acquiring these new things. An example of the first is people will watch 'better' players playing and decide they need to acquire a better backhand. They then think that to acquire it they need a few lessons. Fair enough.

Identifying what needs to be improved and how to improve it is a rapid process. We don't really think or reflect on it; we are not conscious of it. We don't even think about the 'process', rather we head straight for the 'content'; the "What?". From this, we naturally start to think where we fall short and what we will need to do to become 'better'. The question here though should be "Fall short of what?" What is it that determines what I should be doing? So when I decide I need to acquire a 'better' backhand, what is it that causes me to make that judgement of 'betterness' and of me and my current state of inadequacy?

It presupposes what 'good' is

I think that alongside *identifying, acquiring* and *going about* what needs to be improved there is a third factor. I think we seamlessly and unconsciously move towards identifying what we want to improve so rapidly because there is a concept that we already have that facilitates this almost instant or simultaneous transition. The 'concept' (and I'll call it a 'concept' temporarily) I am talking about is the ***form*** of '***The Good***'. We have a formulation in our minds of what a good player is. This is not simply a ***belief***, it is an abstraction that we refer to time and time again in tennis.

Our formulation of 'the good player' will have a direct impact on what we determine what we *identify* as needing improvement. This effect on identifying what we need to improve, has a causal effect on what we think we need to acquire and how we are going to go about improving.

This form constitutes both our perception of it and our interaction with it.

Andy Murray is a 'good' shot maker but at the same time he is a 'good' match player. We can at least attempt to participate in the good shot maker paradigm of Andy Murray. This is the 'good' about Andy Murray that has our attention. We don't just 'believe' Andy Murray is good because he is a good shot maker. Being a good shot maker is what makes Andy Murray a good tennis player. I mean, how obvious is that? But this paradigm of Andy being good because of his good shots has a huge impact on the way we start to *form conceptually* what a good player is.

The first of these is that they need to do something fairly dramatic. We love drama. Tennis on television is discussed in terms of drama. Look at the replays of points. Naturally, the spectacular shots are replayed. Add to this the fact that tennis players are discussed as 'Superhuman'. They are fast, flexible and mentally strong. So in order to improve we need to acquire at least some of these attributes. Improvement and becoming better in tennis is seen very much in these terms. We need to do 'more' to be better.

The 'Loop'

Having better shots and becoming fitter and faster *will* help you play better tennis. These are skills and attributes you can develop and you can 'acquire'. Having 'better' shots will improve your game. Training hard will also *improve* your game ***if*** you believe that having great shots is the main route to improvement. People are often very keen to take lessons. The more lessons I have, the better my shots will become and the more I will improve. I have more lessons, my shots get 'better' and my shots improve. The problem with the *'improvement by building better shots'* model is that we get stuck in a *'loop'*.

I see 'the loop' in action all the time as a coach. I see 'the loop' in action on tennis channels on Youtube. I hear 'the loop' being discussed on TV. The next time you are watching a tennis match on TV, observe what shots are replayed and how they are discussed. You'll see that it is the great and spectacular shots that are replayed. Even more seductively, the commentators assert time and again that it is ***because*** of these brilliant shots that the player is so good. Given that our normal player is watching this spectacle, let's take a look at what might be happening when our player goes for a tennis lesson.

It is my experience that a tennis player will have formed certain beliefs about how tennis is played before they have spoken to a coach. When I receive calls to coach a player, I always ask them what they want to achieve. In almost every case they tell me they want to "improve their shots" **AND THEN** play matches. The *'AND THEN play matches'* reveals two important beliefs that keep people stuck in *the loop*.

The first belief is one that we have looked at before, better shots will 'improve' me as a 'player'. But there is an additional and very important element here and this is the second belief. The first belief is often based on an assumption that *improvement* occurs *separately* from playing points. So already there is a 'decoupling' in a player's head between playing points and *improvement*. Improvement is made 'away' from matches and playing points, during 'coaching sessions'. It is made *prior* to playing a match.

It used to be quite common for players to focus their time and energy on winning matches. They paid little or no attention to technique *outside* of matches. It is quite hard to describe a time in the 1970's and 80's when 'improvement' was seen in a completely different way. To put it bluntly, tactics were prized over technique. Tactics were also prized over physical fitness.

Here is a tantalizing thought. Technique is about YOU–Tactics are about THEM (the other person). Focusing almost exclusively on 'you' seems to make sense. "What is the problem here?" you may ask. I would say that first and foremost,

The loop is deeply embedded in the culture of our sport and is continually being reinforced on TV, the internet and by coaches. I think this has an impact on our perception of what it is to be a good player and what we may need to do to become one.

Some common beliefs

Is it just a case of application?
"All you need to do is apply it in a match"
"Good technique is important"

The Right Order

It is not that these beliefs are wrong, it is that they are in the wrong order. A better way of putting it is that these beliefs are not based on the real reason 'WHY' good players are good players. There are fundamental and foundational reasons why players are 'good'. Good players are good players not because of their great shots and fitness. Great shots and fitness are more like 'symptoms' of being good players but they are not the cause of 'good play'. Understanding what makes a good player will help resolve this problem. Once a player understands these fundamentals, they will be able to make far better decisions on how to improve.

5. Combinatorial Explosion in Tennis: The Complexity of Playing a Match

Tennis is a captivating sport that requires not only physical prowess but also strategic thinking and mental agility. While the basic objective of tennis seems simple, the execution of each shot, the positioning on the court, and the decision-making involved can quickly lead to a phenomenon known as *combinatorial explosion*. This essay explores the concept of combinatorial explosion in the context of playing a tennis match, highlighting the complex and intricate nature of the sport.

Understanding Combinatorial Explosion

Combinatorial explosion refers to the exponential increase in possibilities or outcomes as the number of choices or variables in a given situation increases. In the context of tennis, this explosion arises due to the numerous combinations of shots, court positioning, and strategic choices available to players throughout a match. A player must make split-second decisions based on various factors, such as the opponent's positioning, shot selection, court conditions, and personal playing style.

Shot Selection and Combinations

In tennis, a player has multiple shot options at their disposal, including forehand, backhand, slice, topspin, and volleys. When faced with a shot, a player must consider the trajectory, spin, speed, and directional angle required to play it effectively. Moreover, the combination of shots is vital to constructing effective point-winning strategies. Players must choose the right shot for each situation, considering factors such as court positioning, opponent's strengths and weaknesses, and the desired outcome of the point.

Court Positioning and Movement

One of the most important elements contributing to combinatorial explosion in tennis is court positioning. A player must constantly analyse their own positioning in relation to the ball, the opponent, and the optimal recovery areas of the court. The decision to move forward, stay back, or approach the net depends on factors like shot selection, opponent's position, and the player's own strengths. Each position change introduces new possibilities and further compounds the complexity of decision-making during a match.

Strategic Choices and Adaptability

Strategic thinking plays a crucial role in tennis, adding another layer of complexity. Players must adapt their tactics based on their opponent's playing style, strengths, and weaknesses. They need to consider a range of strategies, such as aggressive baseline play, attacking the net, using drop shots, or employing defensive tactics. The ability to anticipate an opponent's moves, adjust one's game plan, and react swiftly to changing situations is essential for success on the court.

Managing Complexity

Given the inherent complexity and combinatorial explosion in tennis, players must develop various skills and techniques to manage this complexity effectively. This includes honing their decision-making abilities, enhancing shot selection, improving court awareness, and developing strategic thinking. Regular practice, match experience, and analyzing opponents' gameplay are crucial components in understanding and managing the complexities of tennis.

The Pitfall of Combinatorial Explosion: Getting Lost on the Court

While combinatorial explosion in tennis offers an array of possibilities, it can also present challenges for players. In the midst of a fast-paced match, the sheer number of choices and combinations can overwhelm a player, leading to a phenomenon known as getting "lost" on the court.

When a player becomes lost, they struggle to make decisions promptly, leading to hesitation, indecisiveness, and potentially poor shot selection. The vast number of shot options, court positioning considerations, and strategic choices can become paralyzing, hindering the player's ability to execute their game plan effectively.

The pressure of the moment combined with the complexity of the game can amplify the feeling of being lost. As players analyze various possibilities and try to predict their opponent's moves, the mental burden can become overwhelming, causing a player to lose focus and clarity. In this state, decision-making becomes fragmented, leading to a loss of momentum and ultimately affecting the player's performance.

Moreover, the physical demands of tennis add another layer of complexity to the situation. Fatigue can further compound the challenges of combinatorial explosion, as the player's physical abilities and mental acuity begin to diminish. In such circumstances, even simple decisions can feel insurmountable, resulting in a downward spiral of confusion and frustration.

To reduce the risk of getting lost, players must cultivate mental resilience and develop effective coping strategies. This includes training their minds to process information quickly, continually reset their thoughts to the present moment, and maintain a clear game plan. Additionally, having a reliable coach or mentor who can provide guidance and help navigate the complexities of the game can be invaluable in preventing a player from becoming overwhelmed.

Experiencing the feeling of being lost on the court is not uncommon in tennis, particularly for players at various skill levels. However, through experience, practice, and the development of mental fortitude, players can learn to manage combinatorial explosion successfully and regain their composure during matches.

Combinatorial explosion in tennis presents players with numerous possibilities and challenges. While it offers opportunities for creativity and strategic play, it can also lead to players getting lost on the court. The overwhelming number of choices and combinations can hinder decision-making, cause hesitation, and affect overall performance. However, with mental resilience, focus, and experience, players can navigate the complexities of the sport by minimizing the risk of becoming lost and maximizing their chances of success on the tennis court.

Conclusion

Playing a tennis match is a prime example of combinatorial explosion, where the myriad possibilities for shot selection, court positioning, and strategic choices combine to create a highly complex sport. To succeed, players must master the art of decision-making, constantly adapt their strategies, and exhibit mental agility on the court. Tennis truly exemplifies the balance between physical prowess and mental acuity, captivating players and spectators alike with its dynamic and complex nature.

6. Encoded Specificity: Unravelling the Secrets of Memory Retrieval

Memory, the ability to retain and retrieve information, is a fundamental cognitive process that shapes our experiences and guides our actions. Over the years, researchers have dedicated significant efforts to unraveling the complex workings of memory. One influential theory that has emerged is the concept of encoding specificity, which suggests that the effectiveness of memory retrieval is closely tied to the ***context*** in which the information is encoded. This essay explores the principle of encoding specificity, its theoretical underpinnings, and its implications for understanding human memory.

Understanding Encoding Specificity

Encoding specificity theory, proposed by Endel Tulving and Geoffrey R. Loftus in the 1970s, posits that *memory is most effective when retrieval cues match the conditions present during encoding*. In other words, the context in which information is initially learned acts as a powerful cue for subsequent retrieval. Encoding specificity theory challenges the earlier assumption of memory as a purely "storage and retrieval" process and emphasizes the significance of the relationship between encoding and retrieval processes.

Context-Dependent Memory

One aspect of encoding specificity is context-dependent memory, which suggests that the retrieval of information is enhanced when the external environment during recall matches that of the encoding phase. Classic experiments by Godden and Baddeley (1975) demonstrated that participants who learned and were tested in the same underwater environment performed better compared to those who learned and were tested in different contexts. These findings highlight the role of the environment in facilitating memory retrieval.

State-Dependent Memory

In addition to the external context, encoding specificity also extends to internal states. State-dependent memory proposes that the physiological and emotional states experienced during encoding can influence memory retrieval. Research has shown that individuals are more likely to recall information when their mood or physiological state at the time of encoding matches that during retrieval. For instance, if a person learns information while in a happy state, they are more likely to remember it if they are in a similar emotional state when attempting to recall.

Application and Real-World Implications

The concept of encoding specificity has significant implications across various domains. *In educational settings, understanding the impact of context on memory retrieval can guide instructional practices*. By providing students with retrieval cues similar to those experienced during encoding, such as recreating the classroom environment, educators can potentially enhance learning and recall.

In legal contexts, encoding specificity can influence the reliability of eyewitness testimony. The environment in which a crime is witnessed and subsequently recalled may impact the accuracy of the testimony. Legal professionals should be aware of the potential impact of context-dependent memory and consider it when evaluating witness statements.

Moreover, encoding specificity has implications for improving individual memory performance. By consciously manipulating environmental or internal cues during encoding and retrieval, individuals can enhance their memory recall. Techniques such as mnemonic devices, context reinstatement, and mood induction can help individuals align the conditions at retrieval with those present during encoding, thereby boosting memory performance.

Conclusion

Encoding specificity is a fascinating concept that sheds light on the intricate nature of human memory. *The theory emphasizes the importance of context, both external and internal, in facilitating memory retrieval*. Understanding encoding specificity can aid educators, legal professionals, and individuals in optimizing memory recall by incorporating appropriate cues during the learning and retrieval processes. As research in cognitive psychology continues to advance, encoding specificity will undoubtedly remain a valuable framework for comprehending the complexities of memory formation and retrieval.

7. Parasitic Processing Part 1

When what is 'Good' works against you

At its most fundamental, Parasitic Processing occurs when something Good turns bad. Something 'Good' here is *human cognitive function*. Human cognitive function negotiates the infinitesimally large problem space we are confronted with everytime we do something and provides an outcome. Basically, it's amazing stuff. It can, however , work against us. One of the ways that it does so is called Parasitic Processing. Your amazing cognitive functioning works against you and forces you to conclude "I'm doomed". I will argue in this chapter that Parasitic Processing is a 'perennial Problem'. I mean it is perennial in the sense that it can happen at anytime (like some forms of depression) and does happen all the time (unlike depression). This dual combination of both *can* and *does* is my definition of a perennial problem.

Instances of Parasitic Processing are infinitely diverse. Responses to Parasitic Processing are infinitely diverse. Instances and Responses to Parasitic Processing match the infinite size of the 'problem space'. What

I am looking for, in this chapter, are what is universally true of Parasitic Processing and then what the characteristics of Parasitic Processing are. I then want to look at, first, why I think it can help you directly just by having some understanding of it. Second, the different forms it can take and the different ways that it can operate.

A 'theory' of negotiating pressure?

People react to pressure in different ways. Some are able to continue to work under pressure and produce good work. Others can work under pressure and produce bad work. Some people, if pressure is removed, will not perform as well and make mistakes. Some like pressure and others don't. It's a very mixed bag. This is why there is no single answer to 'How do I deal with pressure?' Attempts to do so appear wooden and unsatisfying. Meditation works for some and not for others

I think it is worth noting that just because techniques like meditation do not help 'everyone', it does not mean they do not help someone. People will often do the same things for different reasons and they do these things expecting different desired results. Mediation is a good example. Some meditate to have some respite from the world and to 'heal'. Others do so because they want to gain clarity before tackling the problems of the day. One will expect more healing and the other will expect more clarity.

People also do the same things for the same reasons and expect the same results. Being hypnotized to give up smoking is an example. People go to hypnosis (same thing) to give up smoking (same reason) and aim not to smoke (same desired result). This approach can be expanded and can include the same or different context.

There is no shortage of literature and advice on how to deal with pressure. In my experience, the vast majority of this output looks at dealing with pressure in one, single, linear way. It is often done in the way I mentioned above. Same thing, same reason and same desired result. So the hypnosis to give up smoking example is almost exclusively the xxxx approach.

Parasitic Processing Time & Replication

Parasitic Processing can occur instantly. This means the whole thing from "That's bad", to "I'm doomed" appears to happen in a split second. As we will see with our tennis player, the processing of our opponent's winner as 'bad' leads us to think we are going to lose the match; it happens in a split second. Parasitic Processing can also happen over a longer period of time. We receive an email at 8.35am and we interpret it as 'bad'. In this instance we can go into instant Parasitic Processing or we can go into Parasitic Processing throughout the day. Once the email is treated as 'bad' the 'heuristics' start acting with the 'encoding specificity' and by 9.30 we are working with confirmation bias. By midday, we have started to assume that the probability of something going wrong is very high even though it's at least as low as it was before we received the

email at 8.35am. By 1pm, anxiety started to develop. By 2pm we have lost some cognitive flexibility and reciprocal narrowing has occurred. At this point, we can think of very little else other than the contents of the bad email. By 4pm we think we are doomed.

Once the Parasitic Processing circuit has occurred once, either instantaneously or over time, several things can happen. First, it can stop. This is quite common and is obviously a desirable outcome. The stopping of Parasitic Processing can happen spontaneously, without our input and sometimes as the result of other good news that acts as a counter.

Second, it can keep going and reproduce itself. In this instance Parasitic Processing will continue but it will also grow alongside a general narrative of "I'm doomed". For example with the tennis player, they will interpret the next winner from their opponent as another example of their inadequacy and increased likelihood of losing. They will also treat any winners they make as 'lucky' or 'insufficient' thus extracting and feeding in more examples from the heuristic/encoding specificity loop.

So any winners you make are not treated as a counter (and a potential weapon to end the current cycle of Parasitic Processing). Instead, they are seen as yet more examples of 'bad' things on a par with your opponents winning shots. When even your good shots are seen in a negative light. This is one of the paradoxes of Parasitic Processing and it is a very good sign that you are undergoing Parasitic Processing. In Buddhist circles, it is called 'entrapment'. One of the fascinating features of Parasitic Processing is that you cannot process positives as positive when you are in a negative frame of mind. To use another example (and you can try it now), you can't think of happy things when you are sad. In fact, it never occurs to you to do so. Conversely, it is very hard to remember being sad when you are happy, should it occur to you to do so.

Parasitic Processing and people's responses

We will respond to Parasitic Processing in different ways. We will also respond to different types of Parasitic Processing in different ways. As I mentioned above, we can also respond to Parasitic Processing in remarkably similar ways.

The fact that we do react in similar ways allows us to conceptualize what Parasitic Processing is. The important part of Parasitic Processing that I want to get across is that it is *inevitable*. It doesn't matter who you are, what you do or how you think, it's going to happen. What I have seen with people is that they can soften the effects of Parasitic Processing and that some people are naturally better at doing this than others. Regardless, a response to Parasitic Processing can be cultivated if you think it's necessary. This response can be rehearsed and practiced in real life situations. I want to use x2 examples. We will take our tennis player who has a relentless barrage of Parasitic Processing opportunities during the match and compare it to our person who received a bad email at 8.35am in the example above.

With the tennis player, the response can go one of two ways. The player experiences Parasitic Processing when their opponent hits a winner and

Parasitic Processing carries on into the next point. Here, even if the player wins the next point, they will experience it as a temporary respite on their path to general failure and losing the match. They will also see it paradoxically as another example of them being doomed. Here lies another threat from parasitic processing. A 'General Narrative' begins to form. In other words a *story* begins to develop. This reinforces the individual instances of Parasitic Processing that are taking place point to point.

Below are x2 diagrams that look at how Parasitic Processing functions point to point in a tennis match.

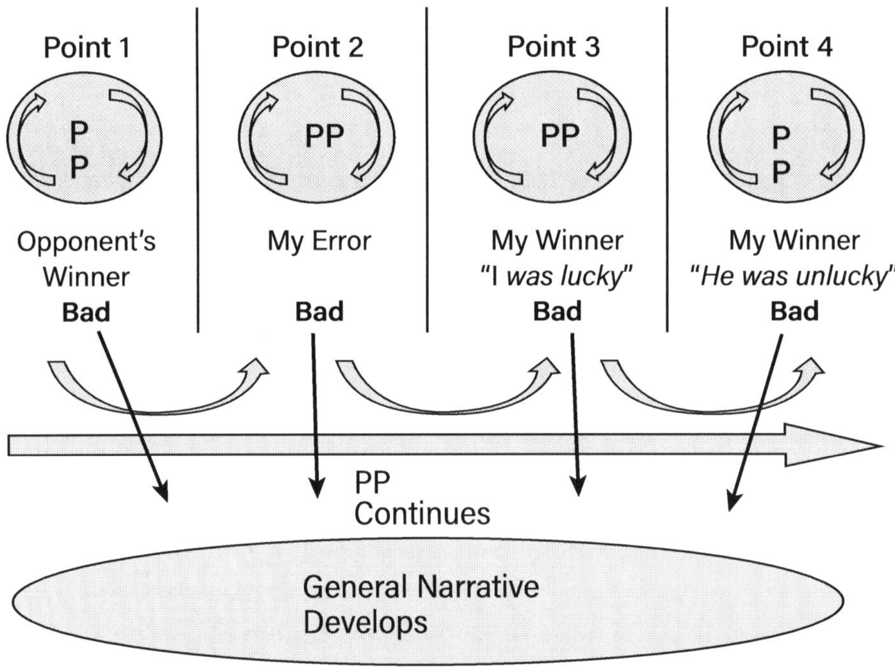

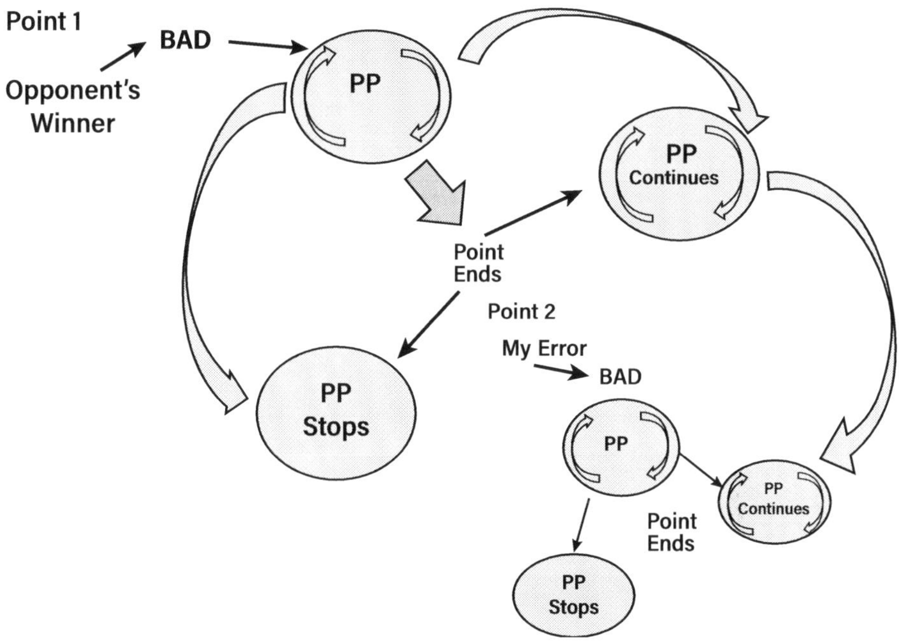

Developing an 'awareness'

In order to cultivate a better way of dealing with pressure, we need to develop an awareness of how our normal cognitive function can work against us and does so without us realizing what is happening. In the case of parasitic processing, we assess probability as high when, in reality, it's low. This leads to anxiety, contradiction and error.

An important part of developing an awareness of how our normal cognitive function can work against us is to develop an understanding of Parasitic Processing. Please note that this is different from trying to correct Parasitic Processing, to cure ourselves of Parasitic Processing or to find a solution.

Understanding Parasitic Processing and how it works can help soften the effects of Parasitic Processing. We can also become conscious of Parasitic Processing is better than trying to find a cure. This is because a 'cure' will always fail. Parasitic Processing will always come back and we will not cultivate our response. With our tennis player example, we have the advantage of the next point to try and reset our thinking and keep our cognitive flexibility.

We have to accept that when we see something as 'bad', we will think of other bad things and think the probability that something bad is going to happen again is higher than it actually is.

There are several problems with Parasitic processing if it develops unchecked. My suggestion is they block anagogue, prevent flexibility and severely limit your ability to deal with problems.

8. Parasitic Processing Part 2

For our purposes of thinking better under pressure we now turn to instructive figures from history. The Buddha reveals an important aspect of the human condition with regards to our problem solving and internal monologues. As, in a sense, we are constantly under threat from our cognitive system going wrong, we would do well to ask the foundational questions of Buddist faith to help address this issue. These questions are encapsulated below:

"What is the Buddha enlightened about?"

"What does the Buddha now know that we don't?"

"What kind of transformation is being brought about by enlightenment?"

In our problem solving framework the above questions relate to enlightenment in the following respects. The cognitive system that allows us to function as human beings can work against us, can damage us. This threat has been called, in the academic domain where cognitive science meets philosophy: 'Parasitic Processing'. This threat is perennial, it is ever present and can be triggered at any time. Parasitic Processing contains within it the process of 'Reciprocal Narrowing' (A contributing if not definitive factor in addiction). Reciprocal narrowing is the mirror opposite of Anagogic Expansion (roughly equivalent to enlightenment).

In order to show us how to set ourselves on the path to enlightenment, the Buddha talks of suffering. He does not mean suffering in the sense of experiencing pain. Buddha's suffering is to 'undergo'. So I can be said to be suffering if I am ill or in pain but I can also suffer ecstasy or joy. The Buddha is trying to 'provoke' us into realizing that our suffering (Dukka) is our loss of agency. This suffering can be described as the process of reciprocal narrowing where we have less freedom to choose and our flexibility of thought constricts.

Parasitic processing is parasitic on the cognition process. When we interpret something as 'bad' it can trigger a process of thoughts and thinking that leads us very quickly through confirmation bias, into anxiety and finally to thinking 'I'm doomed'. As you can probably guess, this process is circular and feeds into itself, the 'host' for the parasite is our own cognitive process. Parasitic Processing can happen almost instantaneously or can take a little more time. The point is it kicks in the moment we perceive a phenomena to be 'bad'.

Recognising what Parasitic Processing is and how it works is important because it shows us how interventions into the process (interventions that will be familiar to everyone), do not appear to work, however hard we may try. For instance, trying to think more positively to counter Parasitic Processing, only makes it worse. In a similar way, 'knowing' that we are vulnerable to 'confirmation bias' and to try and consciously intervene is not going to help us overcome Parasitic Processing. With any of the usual interventions into Parasitic Processing, the system simply reorganizes itself.

For this reason in this chapter, I want to look at the 'Process' part of Parasitic Processing and how we can successfully intervene into and break its damaging cycle. How it works and why it's bad. I then want to suggest where we should be looking to prevent harmful perennial problems like Parasitic Processing from taking place. In finding ways to deal with Parasitic Processing, we can set ourselves on the path to use problems in a completely different way.

Parasitic Processing

Parasitic Processing is a process that has been identified and popularized by John Vervake and Leo Ferraro. In particular, it is Lecture 13 from John Vervake's profound and increasingly influential series *Awakening from the Meaning Crisis* that I have to thank for bringing this concept to my attention and allowing me to incorporate it into my work.[23]

We are going to take a look at Parasitic Processing itself. It would be a good idea to use the diagram below as a guide. I have tried to trace the thought process of parasitic processing as a sequence of individual thoughts eg "It's bad". I must admit, representing Parasitic Processing is quite a challenge and we are finding new ways of doing this all the time. I hope that the following acts as a guide.

I have represented Parasitic Processing as sequential as this is the only way of taking us through each move. I ask you, however, to use your imagination and see the 'moves' in Parasitic Processing as happening ***simultaneously.*** Parasitic Processing is so powerful (destructive) *because* it happens simultaneously. Again, its power is derived from two characteristics. The first is that it is established simultaneously by a single instance of "It's bad" (see diagram below). The second is that once established, Parasitic Processing is augmented by each new instance of *"It's bad"*.

23 *"Relevance, Meaning and the Cognitive Science of Wisdom"* (John Vervaeke and Leo Ferraro) from the book *The Scientific Study of Personal Wisdom* (pp.21-51).

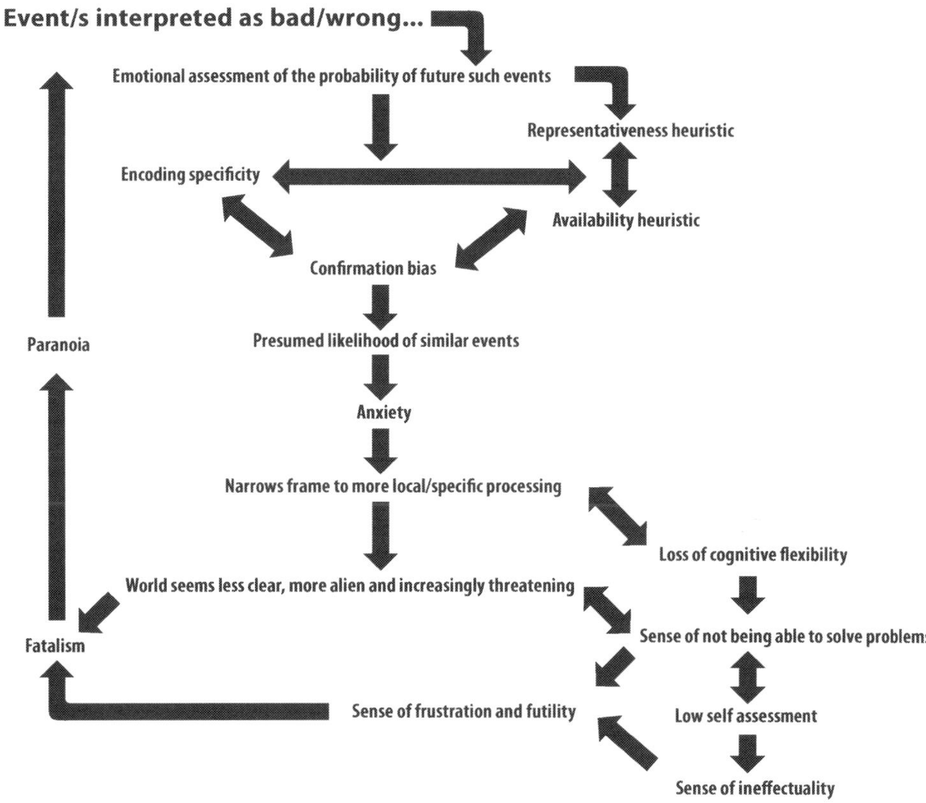

The Process and Significant Moves in Parasitic Processing

Move 1–"It's Bad"

This is where Parasitic Processing starts. We see an event as 'bad'. I am going to use tennis as my example as it's here I have most experience of Parasitic Processing. There are two types of *"It's bad"* in tennis. One group of 'badness' is my opponent's winning shots. The 'bad' here is that my opponent has hit a winner. It is this classification of judgements in tennis that I will use to illustrate the process of Parasitic Processing in this chapter. The other group is my errors. The response to my errors are 'equals' to my opponent's winning shots as instigators of Parasitic Processing. So, our opponent hits a winner; what happens next?

Move 2–"That's bad too"

After Move 1 "That's bad", your brain will try and assess the *probability* of something bad happening again. Assessing probabilities is central to our cognitive function. We do it automatically and we do it all the time. The challenge our cognitive system faces is that the problem space is huge (as good as infinite). Here we face the problem of 'Combinatorial Explosion'.

The problem space is so large we can't negotiate it at all. The number of variables is so great. The number of variables that need to be processed and integrated is far more than the conscious mind can handle. So you use what are called ***heuristics*** *to make implicit calculations. Heuristics are mental shortcuts, typically inculcated by evolution, that help us cut through and zero in on the relevant data when facing a complex problem or incomplete information.*

Taken from: Parasitic Processing–The Cognitive Science of Overthinking. Published: February 24, 2021

The heuristics are essential in assessing probability. In this case we will look at two key players. 1) The *Representative Heuristic* and 2) The *Availability Heuristic.*

The Representative Heuristic

You judge how probable an event is by how *prototypical* it is, how much it stands out. In our case, our opponent hits a winner. He now becomes a player who hits winners at will. He represents a good player. In comparison, I feel that I'm not as good as he is because I don't have the skills and characteristics to hit as many winners. In fact, he hits them with ease and I would have to struggle to do the same. The truth, however, might be that my opponent is not representative of a 'better player' and that he may well make more errors than hit winners (which is nearly always the case in tennis).

The winners this person hits, however, are not representative of reality at all and are, in fact, a distortion of it. We are continually indoctrinated in tennis to think that a 'good' tennis player hits the most winners or that matches are won by the greater numbers of winners that are hit. It escalates. We believe that the more spectacular shots and winners hit by a player are *representative* of 'Good Players'. That it is the winners themselves that make' good' players. The winners 'stand out' and distort our perception of reality.

The Availability Heuristic

The next heuristic that interacts with the representativeness heuristic is the ***availability heuristic***. You judge how probable an event is by how easily you can remember or imagine a similar event occurring. So for our tennis player, it gets worse. After our opponent hits a winner, we can easily imagine them hitting a lot more winners and winning the match. Because we can *easily imagine* them hitting more winners, we will instantly assess the probability of something bad happening again as 'high'.

To add to our athlete's problems, we also have an inherent ***negativity bias***. Here we give much more psychological weight to bad experiences than good experiences. This leads us into Move 3 and Encoded Memory.

Move 3–Encoding Specificity

The 2 heuristics above do not act alone. They immediately interact with your memory in a particularly problematic fashion. The above heuristics interact with a characteristic of memory called '**Encoding Specificity**'. We need to distinguish between 'memory' and 'memories'. The brain has memory which is the *store* of information. Memory is called upon by various cognitive processes to produce specific memories. In our case, it is the assessment of probability, carried out by heuristics. The heuristics call upon memory to produce memories.

Memory 'stores' memories in specific categories:

1) The State you are in. For example, 'happy' or 'sad'

2) The 'Facts' (as it remembers them)

3) Perspectival & Participatory knowing

Our memories have contextual information encoded in them, which affects the retrieval of those memories. This is the 'coding' part of encoding specificity. The coding in memories is based on the categories above.

In his lecture, John Vervake gives two examples of 'coding' and the way it works.

An experiment shows that students who take a test in the same room where they studied perform better than students that were put in a different room.

"A classic experiment on the encoding specificity principle had participants memorize a set of words in a unique setting. Later, the participants were tested on the word sets, either in the same location they learned the words or a different one. As a result of encoding specificity, the students who took the test in the same place they learned the words were actually able to recall more words (Godden & Baddeley, 1975) than the students who took the test in a new setting. In this instance, the physical context itself provided cues for retrieval. This is why it's good to study for midterms and finals in the same room you'll be taking them in."

Moving back to the tennis example, there will be a specific kind of memory that will be more accessible to you when your opponent hits a winner and you interpret this as 'bad'. The heuristics will retrieve memories associated with that thought and the emotion attached to it. In the case of the winner that has been hit by their opponent, heuristics and memory interact and produce thoughts and emotions related to other times this opponent has lost.

From a personal perspective, it is common for tennis players to report thoughts and emotions correlated to certain triggers. On losing a point, the player will say something like "*Here we go again*". To me, this announcement means that the player has almost instantaneously triggered the probability heuristics and selected memories that reinforce that idea that they are going to lose. This outcome of course then, more often than not, becomes a self-fulfilling prophecy.

Move 4 – Confirmation Bias

The above heuristics interact with encoding specificity. At the same time, they can become intertwined with **confirmation bias** in the sorts of processing we are trying to counter.. Confirmation bias is another heuristic and so is part of our assessment of probability. The 'bias' is our tendency to search for, favour, and recall information that *confirms* our current beliefs. So as you're going through your memories, you'll look for 'data points' that confirm your forming judgment that the "bad outcome" is highly probable. And you won't just imagine one bad outcome. You'll imagine multiple bad outcomes and second-order effects, adding up the probabilities in the process.

The final ingredient in this detrimental chain of processing, is what is called 'Entrapment'. Entrapment is not yet complete but it is becoming almost inevitable.

Move 5 – You can't remember being happy when you're sad

A fascinating and compelling feature of Parasitic Processing, particularly in its first phase, is that it seems almost impossible to swap one state for another. The example I would use here is that you struggle to feel happy when you are sad. I say struggle, I think it is impossible, because one repels the other.

In the case of our tennis player, a further and equally as interesting phenomena occurs. When the opponent hits the winner, we remember other occasions this has happened and we see the likelihood of this happening again as highly probable. We also struggle to remember the 'good'; in this case, winning. But it becomes equally hard to 'reset' and start the next point afresh or in neutral. In our tennis example, the response to our opponent's winner is carried over to the next point and we are in trouble.

When we have lost the previous point, the probability of our winning the next point actually increases. In order to comprehend the 'REAL PROBABILITY' of winning the next point and not its heuristically generated counterpart, you need to train your thinking. You need to know how to counter the 'entrapment' of Parasitic Processing.

Move 6 – Anxiety and Reciprocal Narrowing

When you begin to conclude that the probability of a "bad outcome" is high, you experience what you call anxiety. This 'bad outcome' for a candidate who has failed in a job interview for instance can be the loss of the next role they apply for, or the next question they encounter in an interview is misread or delivered and so on..

One of the things that anxiety causes you to lose is your cognitive flexibility. Cognitive flexibility is your ability to change what you're thinking about and how you're thinking about it. It resides at the intersection of awareness, adaptability, and confidence. It is this loss of cognitive flexibility that causes big problems for our tennis players.

As you lose your cognitive flexibility, your framing of reality becomes very restricted and rigid. Your mind operates from a place of fear. So your thinking becomes more and more narrow and obsessive.

Possibilities collapse and the number of options in the world start to decline. You find it difficult to see a way out and your problem-solving skills take a major hit. And so, you lose your sense of agency.

This loss of Agency is what Vervakes calls 'Reciprocal Narrowing'. Reciprocal narrowing is the penultimate act before the final curtain comes down, entrapment is complete and Parasitic Processing has firmly taken root.

Move 7–Mistakes, Failure and "I'm doomed"

When your ability to solve problems goes down, you are more likely to make mistakes and fail. Which will then increase your anxiety and reinforce your negative outlook.

As you might have already inferred, this can become a vicious cycle. It feeds on itself. Dr. John Vervaeke aptly labels it **parasitic processing**.

The whole system acts as a parasite and takes up life within you, causing your consciousness to contract. So here the cycle of malfunctioning approaches to challenges in our environment is complete. The following chapters will discuss how to break out of these common cycles.

9. Meaning Exercise–Don't let the 'meaning' of a match be decided for you

When I talk with players about an upcoming match, they will often start by describing what the match *means* to them. Most of the time they will do this before describing what they think they should do in the match itself. So, for example, I was talking with a friend about his upcoming match which was in a week's time. He said,

"This is a really big one for me, it's probably the most important match I've played. He's a player I know I could beat. If I can play my best, I should win. And if I do, I'll move up a league and start to play better players. I went for a few extra lessons just for this match and my coach says with all the effort that I've put in, I'm going to win. A lot of people are talking about it

and they are saying that they would like to come and watch."

If I could pick out one thing that occurs again and again when talking about upcoming matches with players, it is this: Players seem to accept (or not to notice) that the meaning of a match has been forced on them.

So in the example above, my friend was describing a situation where the meaning of the match had been decided by someone else. In this case the meaning seemed to have been decided by the other members of the club and by his coach. So in his mind, the meaning is both 'external' and it is THE (only) meaning the match can have. It is as if he is giving into fate and there is nothing he can do about it.

I think I can offer at least some kind of explanation as to why people accept that the meaning of a match is decided by someone else. Players often seem to be more comfortable with someone else dictating what the match means. I think this happens for two reasons.

First, they don't know that they can choose the meaning of a match. They therefore do not know *how* to choose the meaning of a match or why it is better that they start to understand that choosing your own meaning can be a very healthy capacity to acquire.

Second, players will often not like to take responsibility and develop a kind of defensive mechanism that operates automatically. The end result is the same, players think that the meaning of a match has already been decided for them and that is just the way it is.

What has occurred to me over time is that players will give meaning to a match without realising that they have the capacity to 'choose' the meaning of that match. In other words, we can choose our own meaning.

This is why the 'thought experiment' in the reflection on 'Meaning' can be very helpful. In this exercise you will begin to understand the process of choosing your own meaning. This will also help stop the meaning of a match being determined by someone else.

Two things occur at the same time

1) The process of giving meaning to a match can spiral out of control, and quickly. As we will see in the reflection on 'Drama' we can often become very dramatic or heroic about our forthcoming matches.

2) Just as with a number of other things in life, we sometimes don't recognise that we have a *choice.* We don't even know that a choice is possible. Because we don't know it is possible, it is almost certain that we don't know how to do it.

The more I *want* it, the more likely it is I'll get it

I have often asked myself, "Why do some people 'big up' some matches? It is almost as if they seem to think that the more they want it, the more *motivated* they will be to win.

To put it another way, players seem to think that the more they want to win the more likely it is they will win that match. At the same time, people conclude, if they don't want it enough they won't get it. I see this happen in other areas of life too.

"I must get this house I want because it's going to make my family's life so much better"

"If I win this match, it will allow me to move to the next level"

Some players display little or no outward desire to win a match. You can see how mad this can make parents and coaches. "*You have gotta want it more! At least show some desire to win*!"

Think about it, those who show the most desire to win are praised whilst those who seem more relaxed are overlooked. Here is the interesting thing for me, those who show more desire are no more likely to win than those who show no desire to win.

In fact, at least in my experience, those who show less desire to win will win more often than those who show a high desire to win.

How can this be?

Those with a heightened emotional desire to win and those with a lower rate are both playing a game of tennis where the objectives are the same. The higher the desire to win, the more 'Dramatic and emotional' it can become. The more emotional and dramatic, the less able I am to make the cool, calm and subtle calculations that I will need to win the match.

I hope this will allow you to explore the meaning of a tennis match and study the next three sections on 'Meaning', 'Negotiating pressure' and 'Drama'.

An example of meaning being 'external'

I am sometimes asked by players I work with, *"What does this match mean?"* I have heard other players ask their coach the same thing. Being put in charge of determining the meaning of some else's match can really go to your head. You can sometimes become obsessed with this powerful influence!

"It means this ...." and the coach will give exactly the meaning that he wants.

I hope that you might see that there are other possibilities and that choosing your own meaning is something you can choose more often and empower yourself.

10. The Games

The list of CI Games is available here - Join the Art of Winning Tennis Community www.artofwinningtennis.com

11

List of CIGs

Shot Momentum Games

First Strike Points

- Play a game to 7 or 10 points, one player will Serve the entire game, then rotate Serve to next player, game must be won by a margin of 2 points.
- Each player will earn a "First Strike Point" when they successfully make their First 2 Shots in the court, then players play out the point and a "Winning Point" is earned in addition.
- If a player makes an error on their First 2 Shots, they do not earn a First Strike Point, only a "Winning Point" is earned.
- Doubles Faults are worth 2 points to the Return player.
- Missed Returns are worth 2 points to the Serve player.

First Strike Power Play

- Play game to 10 points, one player will Serve the entire game, then rotate Serve to next player, game must be won by a margin of 2 points.

- Each player will earn a "First Strike Point" when they successfully make their First 2 Shots in the court.
- If a player makes an error on their First 2 Shots, they do not earn a First Strike Point, only a "Winning Point" is earned.
- If the point ends between 5-8 shots (Patterns of Play), then the player who wins the point will keep their First Strike Point, they "steal away" their opponent's First Strike Point, and also earn the Winning Point. The total number of points earned will be 3. If this occurs, we call this a ***Power Play***.
- If the point reaches the Extended Rally stage of the point (9+ shots), both players keep their First Strike Point and then a Winning Point is earned by the winning player.

First Strike Patterns

- Play game to 10 points, each player can earn a First Strike Pattern Point if they successfully hit their target zone on the First 2 Shots.
- One player Serves the entire game, then rotates the Serve to the next player, the game must be won by a margin of 2 points.
- The Serve target zones for Deuce Court are 1-4 and Ad Court are 5-8.
- The S1 and R1 target zones are A,B,C,D in the court.

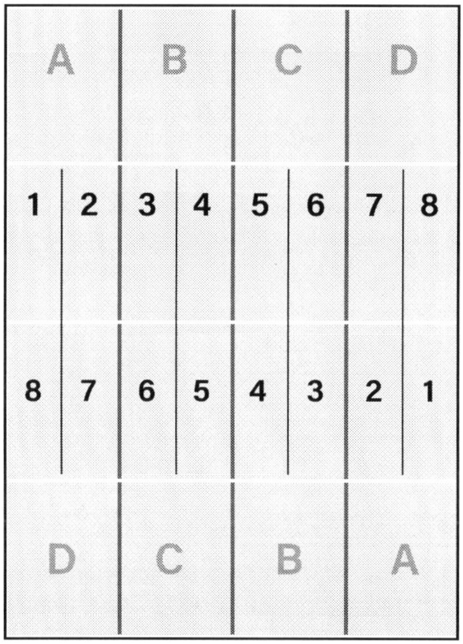

- For example, the Serve player targets for their First 2 Shots would be 4-A, Serve target to 4, S1 target to A. An example for the Return player, Return target is C, R1 target to A.
- Each player earns 1 point for each target hit, for example if the Serve player hits target zone 4 on their Serve and then target zone A on their S1, the player earns 2 points.
- Play out the point until a player wins the point and also earns a "Winning Point".
- Players that hit both targets and win the point can earn a maximum of 3 points.

First Strike Rally Challenge

- This is a warm up game at the beginning of practice.
- Players will not Serve or Return, they will drop underhand feed the point into play from the baseline.

- Play each game to 15 points.
- Decide which player will be the ***First Strike Player (FSP)*** and which player will be the ***Rally Player (RP)***, only the **FSP** player will earn 1 point for every 2 shots in a row they complete during a point, if the **FSP** makes a Net error, 2 points are earned by the **RP.**
- The Rally Player can only earn points from the First Strike Player errors.
- If the RP makes a Net error, 2 points are earned by the FSP.
- If the RP makes a Wide or Deep Error, 1 point is earned by the FSP.
- If the FSP makes a Wide or Deep Error, 1 point is earned by the RP.
- The objective of the First Strike Player is to build consecutive 2-shot sequences consistently during a point without making a Net error (we call this an amateur error because pro players rarely make net errors).
- The objective of the Rally Player is to build consecutive 2-shot sequences and pressure the FSP to make an error.
- Rotate FSP and RP players at the completion of each game.
- Play this game Half Court (Deuce to Deuce) or (Advantage to Advantage), middle 3rd of the court (B and C Zones), you can play full court as well.
- Example scoring: the FSP player makes 4 consecutive shots and misses their 5th shot in the net. The FSP hit 2 x 2 consecutive shots and earned 1 point for each 2-shot sequence, that's 2 points. The Net error gives 2 points to the RP. The Score is 2-2.

Catch 22

- Play a game to 22 points, you can score over 22 points to win the game, you do not have to score exactly 22, however you must win the game by margin of 2 points
- Each player Serves the entire game, then rotates the Serve to the next

player.

- There are 3 stages of a point: First Strike (0-4), Patterns of Play (5-8), Extended Rally (9+).
- If a point ends within the First Strike stage, the winning player earns 2x the number of shots in points. For example, the point ends with a 3 shot rally, the Serve player earns 6 points. If the point is a 4 shot rally, the Return player earns 8 points.
- If a point ends within the Patterns of Play stage, the winning player earns 1.5x the number of shots, rounding up. For example, if the point is a 7 shot rally, the Serve player wins 7 + 3.5 = 11 points.
- If a point ends within the Extended Rally stage, whatever the shot rally length is the number of points earned by the winning player. For example, a 13 shot rally is 13 points, and so on.
- Double Faults by Serve player is 2 points for the Return player.
- Below is a Chart of Point Rally Lengths/Winning Points.

Catch 22

Shot Rally Length	Points Earned
0	**2**
1	**2**
2	**4**
3	**6**
4	**8**
5	**8**
6	**9**
7	**11**
8	**12**
9	9
10	10
11	11
12	12
13	13

Roger That

- Play a game to 10 points, one player will Serve the entire game, then rotate Serve to next player, game must be won by a margin of 2 points.
- Decide which player will be the "Roger That" player, either the Serve or Return player, and which player will be the "First Strike" player.
- If the Serve player is the Roger That player, they must *successfully make the S1 volley in the court to score a Roger That point*. (Serve and Volley).
- If the Serve player is the Roger That player, the Return player is the First Strike player, this means the Return player can earn a First Strike Point (successfully making their first 2-shots in the court).
- The objective for the Serve player is to rehearse their Serve and Volley and be rewarded with a Roger That Point if the volley successfully lands in their opponent's court. The point is then played out and the winning player earns a Winning Point in addition to the Roger That Point (Serve player) or the First Strike Point (Return player).
- At the Art of Winning, we have the players play 2 games when the Serve player is the Roger That player, then 2 games when the Return player is the Roger That player. Play a short set to 4 games or full set to 6 games.
- When the Return player is the Roger That Player, they must *successfully make the R1 volley in the court to score a Roger That point*. (Return and Volley)
- The First Strike player is basically playing the First Strike Points Game (see First Strike Points rules).
- Double Faults are worth 2 points to the Return player, Return errors are 2 points to the Serve player.

Johnny Mac

- Play a game to 10 points, one player will Serve the entire game, then rotate Serve to next player, game must be won by a margin of 2 points.

- Decide which player will be the "Johnny Mac" player, either the Serve or Return player, and which player will be the "First Strike" player.
- If the Serve player is the Johnny Mac player, they must *successfully hit the S1 or S2 approach shot in the court to score a Johnny Mac point*. This is a delayed pressure approach and volley tactic.
- If the Serve player is the Johnny Mac player, the Return player is the First Strike player, this means the Return player can earn a First Strike Point (successfully making their first 2-shots in the court) in each point played.
- The objective for the Serve player is to rehearse delayed pressure approach shots early in the point and be rewarded with a Johnny Mac Point if the approach shot successfully lands in their opponent's court. The point is then played out and the winning player earns a Winning Point in addition to the Johnny Mac Point (Serve player) or the First Strike Point (Return player).
- At the Art of Winning, we have the players play 2 games when the Serve player is the Johnny Mac player, then 2 games when the Return player is the Johnny Mac player. Play a short set to 4 games or full set to 6 games.
- The First Strike player is basically playing the First Strike Point Game, Double Faults are worth 2 points to the Return player, Return errors are 2 points to the Serve player.

SIRI

- Play a game to 7 points, one player will Serve the entire game, then rotate Serve to next player, game must be won by a margin of 2 points.
- Each player will earn a SIRI point if they play a Forehand on the S1 or R1 shot. For the Serve player, this would be a S1 Forehand and the Return player a R1 Forehand.
- The player who wins the point also earns a Winning Point in addition to their SIRI point.
- The objective of the game is for each player to find a Forehand on their

S1 or R1 shot and deny their opponent a S1 or R1 Forehand, then also earn the Winning Point.

Prime

- Play a game to 7 points, one player will Serve the entire game, then rotate Serve to next player, game must be won by a margin of 2 points.
- Each player will earn a Prime point if they play the S1 or R1 shot crosscourt.
- The player who wins the point also earns a Winning Point in addition to their Prime point.
- The objective of the game is for each player to play crosscourt on their 1st shot after the Serve (S1) or the 1st shot after the Return (R1).

Secondo

- Play a game to 7 points, one player will Serve the entire game, then rotate Serve to next player, game must be won by a margin of 2 points.
- The Serve player will earn a Secondo point if they play the S1 shot down the line.
- The Return player will earn a Secondo point if they play the Return (R) or the R1 down the line. The Return player is given the choice to play the R or R1 down the line to earn a Secondo point, they can only earn 1 Secondo point even if they play both the R and R1 down the line.
- The player who wins the point also earns a Winning Point in addition to their Secondo point.
- The objective of the game is for each player to attack down the line in the First Strike stage of the point.

Point Momentum Games

Deuces are Wild

- The Momentum Score is defined as a player winning multiple points consecutively. It can never be a tied score. The Momentum Score is either 1-0, 0-1, 2-0, 0-2, or 3-0, 0-3. The Momentum Score is never scored past 3-0 or 0-3, once it reaches 3-0 or 0-3, it resets back to 0-0. The only time the Momentum Score is 0-0 is the 1st point of the match or when the score reaches 3-0 or 0-3 and then resets back to 0-0.
- The objective of this point momentum game "Deuces are Wild" is simple. The player who wins 2 consecutive points (called a Momentum Point), they win 1 game. The Serve rotates to the next player after 2 points are won consecutively. Once the Serve rotates, in this particular game "Deuces are Wild", the Momentum Score resets to 0-0 to begin the next game.
- First player to score 6 games wins the Set. You must win by a margin of 2 games to win the Set.
- There are no Tiebreaker games played in Deuces are Wild.

Tsunami

- The objective of this game is for players to understand how quickly point momentum can shift from one player to the next.
- Player A wins 2 points consecutively (called a Momentum Point), they win 1 game. The 3rd point (called the Conversion Point) is then played next between Player A and Player B. If Player A who won the Momentum Point then wins the Conversion Point, the 3rd point, Player A wins a bonus 1 game. The Set score is now 2-0 in favor of Player A and the Serve rotates to Player B. The Momentum Score of the next game resets to 0-0.
- If Player A who wins 2 points consecutively (Momentum Point) and

wins 1 game, then plays the next 3rd point (Conversion Point) and loses that point, their opponent Player B "steals" away the Conversion point, The Set score is 1-0 in favor of Player A however the Serve rotates and Player B begins Serving the next game up 1-0 in the Momentum Score.

- Play a Set to 6 games, must win by a margin of 2 games.
- There are no Tiebreaker games played in Tsunami.

Double Mo

- The objective of this momentum game is to highlight that 60% of all games played are won by the player who wins 2 momentum points in the game.
- Players must win 2 momentum points to win the game. This is not 4 points in a row, it is winning 2 consecutive points x 2.
- For example, Player A wins 1 momentum point (2 consecutive points), then Player B wins 1 momentum point. The Player that wins the next momentum point wins the game, a Double Momentum.
- The Momentum score is never tied, a player is either +1 or -1 in the Momentum score.
- Serve rotates to the next player once a Double Momentum is won.
- Play short sets to 4 games or full sets to 6 games, must win by a margin of 2 games.
- There are no Tiebreaker games played in Double Mo.

Conversions

- The objective of this momentum game is to highlight the difficulty in winning the 3rd consecutive point, a Conversion Point.
- Players must win 3 consecutive points to win 1 game.
- Once a Conversion Point is won, the Serve rotates to the next player, Momentum score resets to 0-0.

- Play short sets to 2, 3 or 4 games.
- Players can _only_ Serve a maximum of 10 points, if a Conversion Point is not won then Serve rotates to the next player, Momentum score resets to 0-0.

Wake Up

- The objective of this momentum game is to highlight the importance of winning at least 1 or the first 2 points in a game.
- Play Game scoring, 15-30-40-Game.
- If a player wins the first 2 points of the game and goes up 30-0 (2-0). They win the game automatically. Serve rotates to the next player.
- Players that win the first 2 points of a game (30-0) have a 75% probability of winning the game. Wake Up reminds players of this probability by awarding the game automatically to the player who wins the first 2 points of the game.
- If players each win at least 1 of the first 2 points and the score is 15-15. The game must be played out to completion.
- Games can be played with either Deuce or NoAd scoring.
- Play short sets to 4 or full sets to 6 games.
- There are no Tiebreaker games in Wake Up, the first player who reaches 4 or 6 games wins the Set.

Duck The Deuce

- The objective of this momentum game is to highlight the challenge of sustaining the point momentum in a game.
- Choose which player will begin the Set as the "Duck the Deuce" Player, either the Serve or Return player.
- At the Art of Winning we have players play as the Duck the Deuce player when Serving and Returning. Play 2 games and then rotate the

Duck the Deuce to the next player.

- The Duck the Deuce Player must keep the game score from becoming tied once they have gained the lead, they must "Duck the Deuce". For example, Player A is the Duck the Deuce player and takes the lead in the game score 30-15. If Player B wins the next point and ties the game score at 30-30, Player A loses the game and the Serve rotates to the next player.
- If Player A (Duck the Deuce player) is behind in the game score 15-30, then wins the next point and ties the game score 30-30, the game continues because Player A was behind in the game score, not ahead with the momentum. If Player A goes ahead 40-30, they must win the next point to win the game. If Player B wins the next point and causes the game score to reach 40-40, Player A loses the game.
- The Duck the Deuce player is trying to sustain the momentum when ahead in the game score, they are allowed to come back and tie the game score when behind, however when the Duck the Deuce player is ahead they must win the game before the score becomes tied at Deuce (30-30 or 40-40).

Become the House

- The objective of this point momentum game is to highlight that the player who wins the 1st momentum point of the game has the better probability of winning the game.
- Play game scoring, 15-30-40-Game
- Players are encouraged to keep track of their Momentum Score to help navigate the game score.
- Becoming the House is about becoming the player to score the first momentum point (2 consecutive points) to increase their probability of winning the game.
- 60% of games are won by the player who scores the 1st momentum

point.

- 75% of games are won by the player who wins the first 2 points of the game 30-0 (2-0).
- Play short sets to 4 games or full sets to 6 games.
- There are no Tiebreaker games in Becoming the House.

Flip It

- The objective of this point momentum game is to highlight the difference between the Momentum Path and Conversion Path to win a game.
- The Momentum Path is when a player has to win 2 consecutive points (a Momentum Point) to win the game.
- The Conversion Path is when a player has to win 3 consecutive points (a Conversion Point) to win the game.
- Every game begins with the Game Score 30-30, the objective is to be Player A and win the next point to go ahead 40-30. This means that you are now on the Momentum Path to win the game.
- If you are Player B who loses the point at 30-30 and goes down 30-40 in the game score, you will be on the Conversion Path to win the game.
- Down 30-40, you must win 3 consecutive points (Conversion Path) to win the game.
- If you are Player B, your objective being down in the score 30-40 is to ***Flip the score back*** where you are the player on the Momentum Path to win the game. The way you accomplish this is to win a Momentum Point when you are down in the game score 30-40 and get the score to your ADvantage. At this moment, if you win the Conversion point (3rd consecutive point) and you win the game, fine. However, this is the least probable way to win a game. No worries, if you lose the Conversion Point, you will go back to 40-40 (0-1). This means you have now successfully Flipped back to being on the Momentum Path (winning 2 consecutive points) to win the game.

- The probability of winning the game on the Momentum Path is 75%, the probability of winning the game on the Conversion Path is 60%.
- Play short sets to 4 games or full sets to 6 games.
- There are no Tiebreaker games in Flip It.

30 First

- The objective of this point momentum game is for a player to get to 30 in the Game Score first.
- On average, the player who gets to 30 first in the Game Score has a 60% probability of winning the game.
- Choose which player will be the '30 First' player, then play a short set to 4 games or full set to 6 games.
- If the '30 First' player gets to 30 first, the game continues and plays out to the end.
- If the non '30 First' player gets to 30 first, they win the game and the Serve rotates to the next player.

Court Styles

There are 4 main court styles we have developed at the Art of Winning. Any of the above Competitive Intelligent Games (CI Games) can be played on any of the court styles. In fact, we encourage our players to develop their competitive advantage by using these 4 court styles when rehearsing 2-shot sequence patterns and shot combinations.

First Strike Open Court

- This is the traditional tennis court with adding Serve Position Targets and 4 Court Zones. Players need a court that is designed with intelligent purpose to develop sequenced patterns.

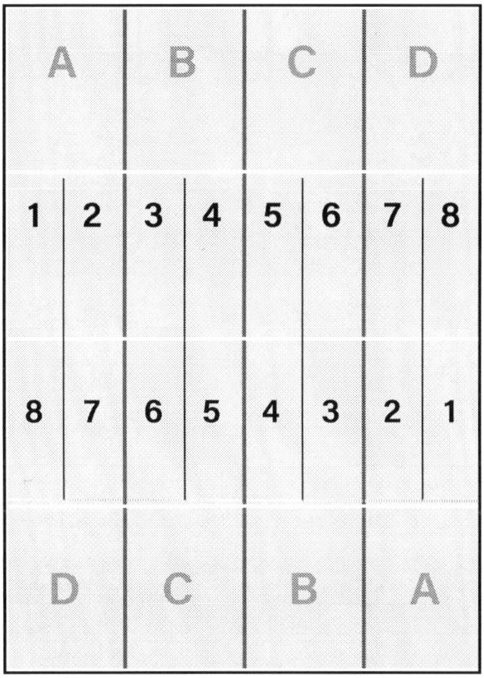

Slim Jim

- The Slim Jim Court consists of Zones B and C, the middle third of the tennis court. This court is designed to develop a player's discipline of playing the ball up the middle and deep into zones that Cage a player. Caging is a term we use at the Art of Winning when a player has to create space and time to send the ball. Typically this involves running around shots that are played right into a player's body. Receiving balls hit up the middle of the court typically keeps an opponent from hitting a sharp angle, however this is a great exercise to develop the skill set of hitting deep from the Zones B or C. Any shot landing in Zone A or D is considered an error.

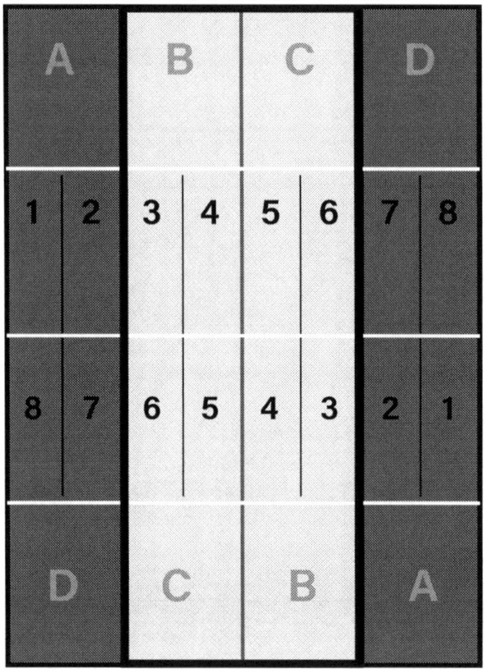

Hurricane

- Hurricane is a court style where a player must play every shot to the outside of the court, Zones A and D. Any shot landing inside Zones B and C is considered an error. This is a difficult court style to master, however the Hurricane court disciplines a player to develop sharp angle shots when receiving sharp angled shots. At the Art of Winning, many times we will allow the First 2 Shots (First Strike Shots) to land in Zones B and C, then beginning with Patterns of Play (5-8 shots), players must play into Zones A or D, the outside of the court.

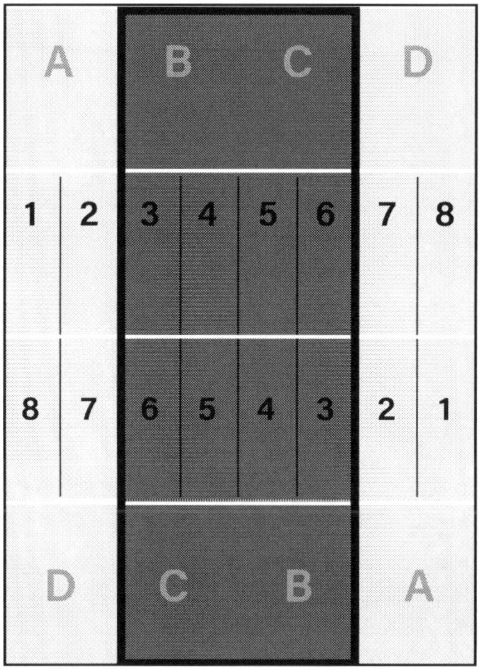

Blackbeard

- Blackbeard is a court style that we developed especially for our junior players because of the temptation to play shots too close to the sidelines. Blackbeard was an English pirate in the 18th Century. The reason it's named Blackbeard is because junior players were complaining about being "hooked" in match play (a term typically used in tennis to describe balls landing close to the sidelines and being called out). The sidelines of the Blackbeard court are 3 feet inside the singles lines, approximately halfway inside of Zones A and D. Any shot landing in the Red Zone is considered an error. The discipline of creating margins of error are paramount to becoming a more competitive player when hitting sharp angles and down the line. Players then begin to understand that they do not necessarily have to hit close to the sidelines to win the point.

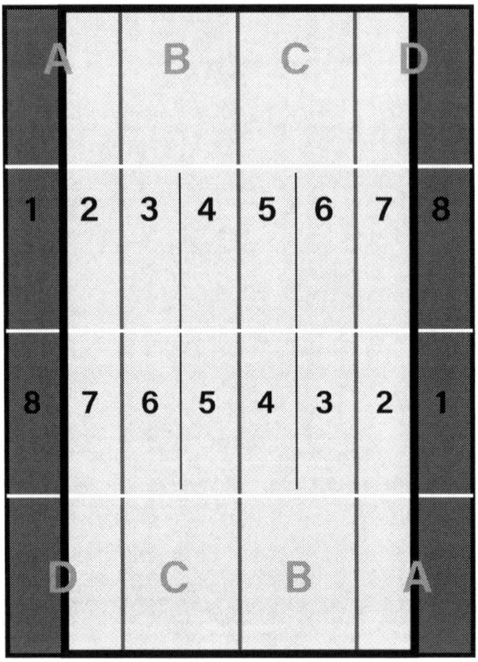
A
B
C
D
1
2
3
4
5
6
7
8
8
7
6
5
4
3
2
1
D
C
B
A

12

The Glossary

Back court zones – There are four zones of the Backcourt A,B,C and D. They are most commonly used to describe the First Strike Patterns.

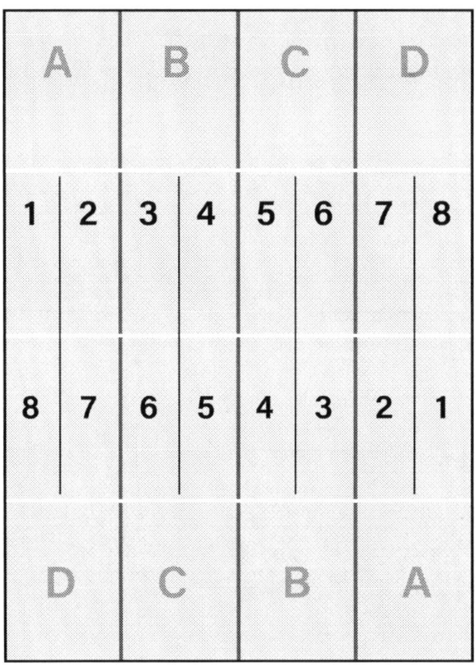

Checking out – Although still in the match, the player is said to have checked out when they have resigned themselves to losing. They may look happier on the outside, almost relieved but they have next to no chance of winning. Checking out of matches is a tendency that a player needs to address and negotiate a process of staying checked in mentally and emotionally.

Closeness – Closeness is a feature of a tennis match. It is a particular feature of the Set. The set in a tennis match is always much closer than a player perceives it to be. This creates what is called the problem of closeness. The problem is twofold: first, the tennis scoring system is deceptive and ultimately misleading; second, players find the closeness uncomfortable. An inability to deal with closeness can encourage players to check out or try and race ahead by hitting unsustainable winners.

Competitive Intelligence – This is a cognitive capacity. It optimizes perception, thought and language by improving each of them simultaneously. By developing Competitive Intelligence, the player stays focused on what is relevant to winning matches. By its use, the capacities of Competitive Intelligence continue to grow and become more durable, flexible and sophisticated.

Conversion point – This is the third consecutive point won by a player; so a Conversion is three points in row.

Direction point – A direction point is the first point a player wins. It precedes a Momentum point.

First Strike – The first two shots a player makes in a point are referred to as the First Strike. The First Strike can be described as the *Sequence* of two shots: for example, S/S1 R/R1. First Strike can also be described as a *Combination:* for example FH / BH (Forehand then Backhand). The First Strike can also be described in terms of where the ball was hit to. This is called a *First Strike Pattern*. Examples of *Patterns* on the serve are: 4–C and 7–A. Examples on the return are: C–C and A–D.

It is critical to note that First Strike does not mean "aggressive on your first 2 shots of the point". This is a major mis-characterization of the term. First Strike can be played in a defensive manner or rally manner.

The First Strike is the stage or phase of the point which encompasses the first four shots of a point between the Serve and Return players (0-4 shots).

First Strike language – When the way we talk about tennis matches is centred on and framed by the first four shots played in a point. First Strike will refer to the S/S1 and R/R1 sequences by specific combinations and patterns of shots as above.

First Strike Combinations – The combination is FH/BH, BH/BH and so on. One of the aims of studying First Strike is to determine the results of specific First Strike combinations.

First Strike Patterns – This describes where the ball was hit to as a sequence of two shots. The serve was hit to Position 4 and the next shot (S1) was hit to C. This would read: S = 4 / S1 = C–then it can be shortened to: 4–C. Other examples of *Patterns* on the Serve are: 3–C and 7–A. Examples on the Return are: C–C and A–D.

The Games – A series of games that are structured to improve the player's First Strike and Momentum scoring capabilities. The Games are the first successful attempt to realistically reproduce the match court on the practice court. The Art of Winning goes further and says that the Games are more matchlike than the match itself. The games are central to developing Competitive Intelligence.

Hidden margin – The small number of points that separates the winner from their opponent: this cannot be detected by either player. This leads to the illusion that the gap between winner and loser is greater than it really is.

Legacy – The outcome of the previous point has an effect on the result of the point to come. The effect of the previous point can be consciously harnessed by the player. For example, they can make a better decision if they take into account the result of the previous point. In this way, the player is using Momentum scoring and probability to make a better decision. Whether or not the player recognizes the legacy it will have an effect on the next point (see Probability).

Momentum point – A momentum point is gained when the player wins two points in a row. Momentum points proceed Direction points and precede Conversion points. Gaining Momentum points first in a game significantly increases the probability of the player winning that game. A player will usually require two Momentum points in order to win the game. Momentum scoring forms an essential part of *The Games.*

Momentum Scoring – This is a scoring system that helps the player negotiate the problem of *Closeness.* It is used to habituate the player into winning two points in a row rather than play to the game score; fifteen all, deuce etc. Momentum scoring consists of: a *Direction point* (One point), a Momentum point (Two consecutive points), a Conversion point (Three points in a row). Momentum scoring acts as a counter to the traditional scoring of the game. While the traditional score is only a point of reference, Momentum scoring takes into account the reality of the game–by making the player conscious of the real patterns, dynamics and probabilities in winning the game.

Point Rally Length (PRL) – The number of shots that successfully land in the court before an error is made. Is one of the categories that form the core of Tennis Data Analytics. PRL data allows you to pinpoint exactly when errors occur. PRL works with the other categories to form what is called the *Story Board of Play.*

Probability – This is measured in percentage and it gives you the probability of winning the next point. Probability is calculated based on the outcome of the previous point and previous Art of Winning Data. This means that the Art of Winning Data Analytics has concluded the following: a player who has lost the previous point has a 60% chance of winning the next point; a player that has won the previous point has a 40% chance of winning the next point and a player that has won the previous two points has a 30% of winning the third and making a conversion. All probability calculations follow the above pattern.

The probability percentages are used in making a decision by the player about the next point. In particular, the player uses the probability percentages to select which First Strike Pattern to play on the next point.

Rally segments – There are three Rally Segments. They are: 0–4; 5–8 and 9 plus. 0–4 = First Strike–5–8 = Patterns of Play–9 plus = Extended Rally.

Repetition illusion – This illusion is one that is central to traditional tennis culture. The illusion is that repetition is an indispensable part of a tennis player's improvement. Repetition on the practice court includes drills and rallying. It tends to exclude the serve and return which forms a strong contrast with *The Games* used by The Art of Winning.

R1–The retuner's next shot after the return (R)

S1–The server's next shot after the serve (S)

Stages between shots

1. Place and time–The player needs to be in the right place at the right time to prevent the ball bouncing twice.
2. Position–The way the body is positioned for optimal delivery.
3. Delivery–The swing and contact produce the hit. There are numerous delivery options including spins, height etc
4. Recovery–After delivery the player looks at the opponent and moves behind the baseline or moves forward. The Recovery stage should be built around the move back into Stage 1.

Service box zones – There are eight service box zones. Together they turn the service box into quarters. The service box zones are targets for the server and produce different responses from the returner.

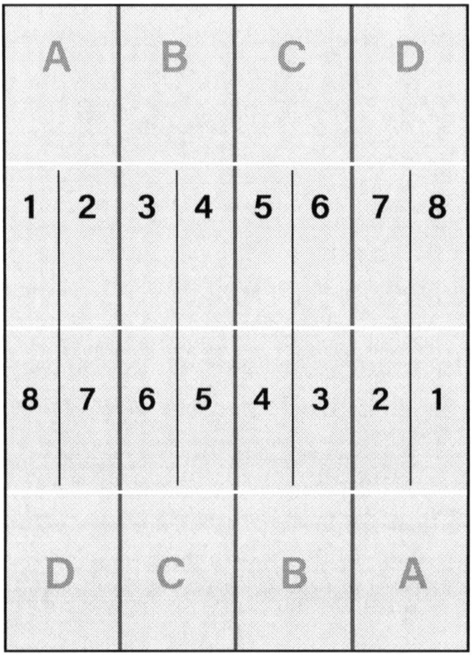

Storyboard of play–When Tennis Data is collected and analysed, patterns can be seen and detected. There will be First Strike Combinations, Patterns and Sequences. These First strike features will combine with Point Rally Length to produce a Storyboard of Play. This is like the narrative of the match but it is much closer to the reality.

The storyboard helps players and coaches focus on what is relevant. It allows the coach and player to talk about the previous match, upcoming matches and what needs to be done on the practice court.

Strong Problem Framing–The ability to look at problems in terms of their context and relevance.

Join the Art of Winning Community

A Free pass into the world of The Art of Winning

www.artofwinningtennis.com

Printed in Great Britain
by Amazon

120d69e7-bb59-4157-b714-b162f2a37f81R01